The Irish Goodbye

ALSO BY BETH ANN FENNELLY

Heating & Cooling

The Tilted World (with Tom Franklin)

Unmentionables

Great with Child: Letters to a Young Mother

Tender Hooks

Open House

THE Irish Goodbye

MICRO-MEMOIRS

Beth Ann Fennelly

W. W. NORTON & COMPANY
Independent Publishers Since 1923

Printed in the United States of America
First Edition

For information about permission to reproduce selections from this book, write to
Permissions, W. W. Norton & Company, Inc., 500 Fifth Avenue, New York, NY 10110

For information about special discounts for bulk purchases, please contact
W. W. Norton Special Sales at specialsales@wwnorton.com or 800-233-4830

Manufacturing by Versa Press
Book design by Patrice Sheridan
Production manager: Ramona Wilkes

ISBN 978-1-324-11740-7

W. W. Norton & Company, Inc., 500 Fifth Avenue, New York, NY 10110
www.wwnorton.com

W. W. Norton & Company Ltd., 15 Carlisle Street, London W1D 3BS

Authorized EU representative: EAS, Mustamäe tee 50, 10621 Tallinn, Estonia

1 2 3 4 5 6 7 8 9 0

In memory of my sister

and in memory

of my mother's memory

Contents

The Irish Goodbye

Married Love: Playing the Long Game

Even now, three years later, when she opens the drawer beside the stove for an oven mitt, she finds the oven mitts folded. This is because, three years earlier, during an intense game of Scattergories, when the category was *Things You Fold* and the letter was O, her husband had written *oven mitts*. "Nobody *folds* oven mitts," she scoffed, and refused him his point, forcing him, ever since, to prove it.

Lori Cornelius

I call Lori Cornelius, thinking I'm calling Lori Hannah. Even though I can clearly see the name on my phone, only when Lori Cornelius answers with her chipper "Hello!" do I realize I've called the wrong person. "How nice to hear from you!" exclaims the very nice Lori Cornelius, whom I haven't seen in a few years. If I were less stressed, I might pretend I'm calling to catch up. Instead, I blurt that I hadn't meant to call her. I moved my mom into her assisted living yesterday, I say, and I've been trying to reach her intake specialist. I explain how my mom is suffering from dementia, and how I'm worried about her, and how, every time I do something stupid like call the wrong person, I worry about my brain too, worry that I'm experiencing the so-called "early signs." Then Lori Cornelius, whom I never intended to phone, tells me she went through the same thing with her mother some years back, and she also began questioning whether she was losing her mind—something, for that matter, she is still questioning—so I might as well get used to it. We laugh and I feel better and we hang up. And now I can relax, knowing that I really *don't* have dementia, because, as it turns out, I really *did* call the right person. Good old Lori Cornelius.

Two Sisters, One Thinner, One Better Dressed

When my sister and I would meet at her apartment before heading out to bars, I would choose my clothes with care. I knew that when I walked through her door, she would study me, especially if a few weeks or more had passed since we'd seen each other. Sisters are envious, sure, but we were also gathering information. We shared a likeness, so it was a way to test how we'd fare in a different outfit, a new haircut. She was often thinner than I was, but I had better style. Younger by two years, I was her leader only in fashion; I would often be wearing something she hadn't yet considered. She would ask me where I got it, and I would tell her, maybe showing off a little. Sometimes she'd want to try it on and I would accessorize her, cuff her jeans or angle the belt on her hips. If she asked, we'd swap outfits for the night. It was worth being the frumpier one to make her happy.

I'm still aware of how I look when I visit her. I live in a different state now, so it's not as often, but when I'm back in Illinois at our mom's house, I always end my run by visiting her. I stand panting in the grass at my sister's feet. I'm aware of how she sees me, huffing clouds from my lungs, my legs strong, my skin bright with sweat in my new running clothes. Still showing off, I suppose, as she's stuck wearing the navy suit I chose the last time I styled her, a suit now thirteen years outdated, though fashionable enough when they closed her casket.

The Stories We Tell About the Stories We Tell

"Fresh laundry!" My husband appeared at the bedroom door, folded T-shirts stacked in his arms.

"Perfect timing."

"How's the packing?"

"Slow going," I said, and smiled. He knew I wasn't eager to leave him and the kids for two weeks.

He deposited the shirts on the bed next to my open suitcase. "Have you decided where you'll spend the long weekend?"

Between the two five-day writing workshops I'd be teaching in Prague, I was free to travel. "Well, Berlin is a short train ride. So is Kraków. And Budapest."

"I thought you were revisiting your old town on the Polish border?" He handed me my pajamas, just out of reach on the bed. "Didn't you write a letter to somebody there?"

"Yeah, my old office mate." I rolled the pajamas, tucked them beside my socks. "She invited me to visit." I began rifling through the T-shirts.

"Then why wouldn't you? Going back at forty-two to where you lived when you were twenty-one—that's some serious closure, right there."

My hands stilled. Why wouldn't I go back? Only because it's the sole place I've lived where I was disliked, thoroughly and impersonally, by almost everyone I met.

In 1993, as my college experience came to a close, I watched my friends fulfill their professional destinies, watched their internships morph into entry-level jobs, watched the prelaw majors level up into law school. This all seemed needlessly practical; while I sensed that a grad program for creative writing might be in my future, first I wanted an adventure. Bonus if this adventure was out of the country; after the "Greed is good" eighties, after the beating of Rodney King on national TV, I wanted to see what else was out there. Somewhere, I had to believe, there must be a country with a moral core, one that valued arts and literature.

The adventure presented itself in the form of a novel profession—teaching English in a former Communist country.

In the years ramping up to my graduation, I'd watched with interest as the Communist bloc began to crumble, first in Poland, then Hungary, then cascading through Eastern Europe, uprisings against totalitarianism. In the Czech Republic, these uprisings appeared especially sexy, as they were led by people my age, students, workers, and actors, inspired by a persecuted poet-philosopher-playwright, Václav Havel. He was forging a nonviolent transition to democracy and the free market. Like the other new entrants to the world economy, the Czech Republic needed to conduct business in English. Hence, they needed English teachers. Well now, I *spoke* English. This could work out nicely. I'd do my part to nurture the Velvet Revolution, help freedom triumph over tyranny. I'd be able to give back a little. And I'd have a bit of a lark while I was at it.

I wrote a letter to the US Embassy in Prague, and I was offered a job at a business college in Silesia, on the Polish border. This region was a slow seven-hour train trip from Prague, but that meant I'd be more needed—already the capital was filling with expats drawn to "the Left Bank of the nineties," its cafés and cobblestones and cheap rent. The relative lack of comforts in Silesia would present more of a challenge, which I figured might inspire my writing. Silesia, which was part of Nazi Germany in World War II, was depressed, industrial, and still heavily Communist. I'd be one of its first native English speakers. I loved that idea, even when I learned another name for the region: the Black Triangle. Coal pollution hung over Silesia like its own iron curtain.

When I arrived in the fall, I'd never taught before, like most "teachers" flocking to Eastern Europe. The arrogance in that stance hadn't yet revealed itself. However, while I would go on to make countless mistakes, I discovered that I loved being in the classroom. So it wasn't the teaching that broke me. Nor was it the fact that I moved to a region with no English speakers while speaking approximately zero words of Czech. I learned Czech in that way you learn if you want to do the little things, like, say, eat. Potatoes, cabbage, garlic, and onions—these words were on quick rotation, for typically those were the only vegetables. At the market, I'd order two of something, or five, because I couldn't pronounce the dreaded *ř*, a sound unique to Czech, found in the words for "three" and "four."

No, it wasn't the teaching or the language. It's that I lived surrounded by people, but in almost total isolation. I'd never experienced loneliness before, had no resources to combat it. Before I left the US, I'd told people I'd be "immersing" myself in Czech culture. My part, I assumed, would be showing up. Oh, it would be hard to find a girl more naive than the one stepping down onto Czech soil with my copy of Hemingway's *A Moveable Feast* and "We Are the World" theme song and the conviction, which had never failed me before, that folks would like me if I smiled hard and tried hard, both skills I'd perfected. Yes, I was a very smiling, very trying girl.

Like one-third of the Czechs, I lived in a prefab concrete *panelák*, apartment buildings that are cheap and fast to assemble. A large grid of them is called an "estate," gray towers endlessly replicated, as if in some apocalyptic mirror. Each panelák is partitioned into identical small apartments—Václav Havel called them "undignified rabbit pens." Their lack of individuality was intentional, designed to foster a collectivist nature, but conversely made residents secretive, yearning for privacy. The thin walls allowed the wardens—all buildings had one—to monitor their neighbors.

Enter one do-gooder American, loitering in the foyer, trying to introduce herself. Everything I knew about making friends wasn't working. My neighbors fell silent whenever I appeared, though I felt their eyes at all times, saw the curtains lift as I trudged to school. If I encountered a neighbor in the concrete stairwell, they'd usually return my "*Dobrý den*," but they wouldn't return my smile or eye contact. The combination, feeling both ignored and scrutinized, unsettled me. This was no "immersion," no lark, no moveable feast, no barbaric yawp to novelize in my future grad program.

I spent my days in silence: I'd rise from bed, sometimes leaving behind on the pillow my head's shape outlined in coal dust. I'd walk to the business college and teach. In the cafeteria, I ate alone—the language barrier was immense, and the students learning English were intimidated when I joined them. Most of my colleagues in the Languages Department spoke English, but I never saw them there, though whether they ate in their offices—everyone kept their office door closed at all times—or ate together elsewhere, I never knew. At four, I'd walk home, the sky already darkening—in the Black Triangle, dusk fell an hour earlier than in the rest of the country. I'd hunch through my "estate" (I can't write that word without scare quotes) to my soul-crushingly ugly building. I'd climb the stairs, swapping the stink of burning coal for the stink of boiled cabbage.

Inside my flat, from the thin-walled bathroom, I could hear couples above and below arguing.

Though no one spoke *to* me, they spoke about me plenty. Because the Czechs couldn't pronounce the *th* consonant cluster in my name, they called me *Americanka*—"American woman"—pronounced "Amera-CHUNK-a." When I shared this with a friend in Amsterdam, he sent a postcard addressed to "Američanka, Silesia." It took three months—I imagined it forwarded from post office to post office, at each, scrutinized for a secret message—until it reached me.

The Czechs were studying me, perplexed, and I was studying them, perplexed. I had questions, but no one to ask. For example: Where were the men? And I didn't mean hotties—I meant men, period. The shops and streets were populated by women. Later, I'd realize that the men there were beneath me, literally, in the mines. And I finally understood why the men wore eyeliner. Coal dust had painted the crevices of their eyes. They worked eighteen-hour shifts, three thousand feet below the surface. The mineshaft elevator took seven minutes to belch them into the world of light. They'd shower, then trudge to a smoky pub and drink, sometimes passing out on the sidewalk after closing. Walking to the college in the morning, I'd step over their legs.

I had no computer, of course—it would be a year before that strange term, the World Wide Web, would be bandied about. And I had no phone. I used the one at the university—no longer bugged, I was told—to call home collect once a month. What did I do with myself? I studied Czech, trying to master the damn ř (a trilled *r* pronounced *at the same time* as the "zuh" of "measure." Go ahead, try. You can't do it either). I wrote letters, mostly to my college roommates, or my Scottish boyfriend, Colin, who was about to dump me. I filled notebooks with maudlin poetry. I tried to learn English well enough to teach it. I dreamt of arugula. I spent weekends so isolated that sometimes, greeting my class Monday, my voice croaked. And I read the same half dozen novels over and over. A typical evening: I finished *War and Peace*, rose from the chair to make tea. After it steeped, I wrung out my tea bag for reuse (living in a poor country taught me thrift. I'd brought three Ziploc bags, and I'd wash and hang them to dry. Even now, I feel a pang when pitching a Ziploc). Then I'd return to the one chair and start another novel.

I was twenty-one, and fun, and pretty, and it didn't seem fair.

When I couldn't take it anymore, I'd take a train to visit Kathleen, my American friend, who was teaching in a lovely cobblestoned university city closer to Prague, and rooming with other English speakers, which is to say, she wasn't nearly so crazy-ass lonely. We sometimes traveled on weekends and shared a lot of laughs, often at the expense of the Czechs, who felt like adversaries to me. Once a bitter, blonde waitress in České Budějovice triple-charged us for our *smažený sýr*—basically a mozzarella stick on steroids—thinking we were dumb Americans. But we were even dumber than she thought: to punish her, we grabbed our parkas and sprinted out the back. Where Blondinka was hiding behind the dumpster. In defeat, we handed over her usurious sum. But Blondinka secreted the money and called the cops anyway. Only some *very* sweet talking kept us from getting deported.

So our laughter was not coming from a place of affection. We smirked at Czech thrift even as we practiced it. We condescended. We traded our students' language errors. (My favorite, harvested from a love letter—my student wrote that I'd given his heart "the fire" but, because I'd rebuffed him, now I gave him "the heart burn.")

We ranked the random window displays of shops that had been confiscated by the Communists, now newly returned to the shop owners' descendants as restitution. (My favorite: a used wedding dress surrounded by car parts.) We joked about *babičkas*, short, square matrons between sixty and ninety, with droopy brown dresses, wool cardigans, kneesocks, and heavy-bottomed shoes. They hawked loogies the size of tea bags, and when the bus pulled to the stop, elbowed everybody out of their way.

None of this is making me sound like a nice person. You're not a nice person if you move to a country to help it transition to free speech and end up poking fun at it whenever two or more are gathered in the name of English. But I couldn't stop myself. My unlikability both wounded and embarrassed me. I felt ill-used by my neighbors and colleagues. Babička-bashing was a release. A short-lived one: too soon, I'd be riding the Sunday evening train back to Silesia. I could tell we were nearing when the buildings started leaning. The mines had so honeycombed the land that it had settled, called "subsidence." Even the *earth* is depressed here, I'd think.

I'd never valued the privilege of living in a beautiful environment until I lived in a place bereft of beauty—in food, in architecture, in aesthetics. I'd never even *considered* the privilege of living in a healthy environment. Sometimes my kitchen tap sputtered brown water. Bottled water was expensive; more expensive than beer. I drank a lot of beer. I've always been a runner, but in Karviná, people stopped to watch. They'd actually *point*. With actual fingers. Furthermore, back from a run, I'd cough black scum onto my palm. It seemed healthier not to exercise. Instead, I ate smažený sýr, putting the "CHUNK" in Američanka.

As the months wore on, sometimes a group of students invited me out for a beer. And my colleagues—Hedvica, who'd once taken a course in England, and Kristýna, head of Languages—gradually became cordial. My office mate, Květa, with her long hippie hair, was more than cordial. She invited me to hear jazz a few times across the border in Poland—jazz, which the Communists had suppressed because it celebrates individual improvisation. Květa was the most natural polyglot I've ever seen. When she was a girl, her sixteen-year-old sister fled Czechoslovakia for France. Ever since, Květa's family had been persecuted. Their apartment was bugged. Young Květa's pen pals in Switzerland and England stopped writing—later she'd realize their letters had been confiscated. Květa's brothers in the army (there was a mandatory conscription) received the worst assignments, the lowest pensions. Her mother's applications for a bigger apartment were rejected. Because of Květa's English—which was probably better than mine—the officials suspected that she, too, would defect. So this woman who spoke five languages with pitch-perfect pronunciation was rejected every single year when requesting a visa to travel abroad.

Květa was the closest I had to a friend. Which wasn't very close. Halfway through my year, we were in our tiny office—our chair-backs almost touching—when I opened a letter from home. Our beloved dog had died. "He was a dog among dogs," wrote my emotionally reserved father. I started weeping, feeling so damn homesick and fearing for my sister—that dog had loved her so much that he'd wait outside the bathroom while she peed. My tears were plopping fatly on my father's expensive stationery. I thought—Why doesn't Květa put her arms around me? My self-pity ratcheted up my sobs—a real drag-your-palm-across-your-snotty-nose-boo-hooing.

Did I think about bailing on my one-year contract, heading home? You bet. I focused on sticking it out until Christmas, which I'd spend with Kathleen. We were invited to share dinner with the family of one of her students. The traditional meal is fried carp, and each family buys their live fish from a barrel and, in the days leading up to the holiday, lets it swim in the bathtub to keep it fresh. My clearest memory of Christmas 1993? Huddling with a nice Czech family in their tiny bathroom as the patriarch held down a flopping carp and hammered it in the head.

So. I'd made it through Christmas. Spring arrived slowly and the weather warmed, and when I woke, I rarely saw my head outlined on the pillow.

There was no thawing with my neighbors, though. One night, sleepless, I lay wondering what my neighborhood looked like before it was bulldozed for paneláks. Probably it had been filled with the same nineteenth-century plaster-walled houses that lined the square.

Then something so terrible rushed into my head that I sat up and grabbed it.

The people who'd lived here: They'd been Jews.

My city was only thirty-seven miles from Auschwitz. It took me some months to realize that, because when Kathleen and I visited Auschwitz we'd gone by bus from Kraków, so the journey had taken several hours. But later I clocked its proximity on a map. I could practically walk there.

So that was the other reason this place was polluted. It wasn't just coal dust. It was ashes.

Before I left, I experienced one last alienation, this time from my conscience: I slept with a student. This was in April, the night I'd learned Kurt Cobain had shot himself. From this distance, I'm embarrassed to admit that the suicide of a rock star could so unhinge me, but I guess the bolts had been falling out all along. After four years of affectionate cuddling with my college roommates, I was starving for touch. Colin had dumped me for good. I hadn't yet learned the psychologists' term for the physical yearning of baby rhesus monkeys separated from their mothers—"skin hunger"—but that's what I had.

I could tell you that the student who took me to his bed was only one year younger, that lots of expat teachers were offering these supplemental English lessons, but even at the time—indeed, even as he unbuttoned my flannel shirt and lowered his warm mouth to my lonesome breasts—I knew it was wrong. My teaching was the sole thing I'd been proud of. No longer. In class Monday morning, I looked at my students' faces, and I knew that they knew.

Finally, it was time to pack. I junked sheaves of overwrought poems. I gave away my exhausted, beloved books and my exhausted, detested clothing.

Květa organized a farewell reception, bread and sausage and mustard and pickles. My colleagues presented me with a gift, a velvet case that popped open to reveal a manicure set, a dozen instruments all hugged to the suede lining by elastic loops. It would have cost them a lot of money, even divided several ways, and I was surprised by it. I was further surprised when Hedvica remarked, "We've always said you have beautiful hands." I didn't recall any of them ever looking straight at me.

I left with less than I'd brought. And a good bit less certain about myself and the world than when I'd arrived.

And now, for the first time, at exactly twice the age, I'd return. I was not only invited back to the country where I was almost deported for stealing fried cheese, I was getting paid, and giving a reading at the US Embassy. I felt a petty vindication, like the girl who gets dumped in high school but awaits her twentieth reunion because she's a CEO and her ex is bald.

In the subsequent twenty-one years, I'd pretty much gotten over feeling disliked by an entire nation: I'd found Tommy. Love can make you more generous. Also, in grad school, I'd found my people, my poetry people. ("See?" I'd imagine telling my Czech detractors. "Not *everybody* dislikes me.") Tommy and I began our family. Loneliness would never again be a problem. Sometimes, at a restaurant, cutting my kids' meat, I'd glance at a woman dining alone, reading a novel, and yearn to swap.

I'd also gained perspective. One frustration of my Czech year was feeling trapped in my ignorance. I had no one to whom I could address my most pressing questions, no newspapers, radio, or TV (I never did confirm whether my "estate" was in the former Jewish quarter. Whom could I have asked?).

Now, I better understood the pressures warping the culture I'd planned on "immersing" myself in. For example, in the 1970s and '80s, the secret police relied on informants. Some had been manipulated, blackmailed, or tortured into collaborating. Some merely desired a job transfer or a travel pass to France. With the dirt these informants provided on dissidents, the secret police "carried out more than 230 executions," according to Amnesty International, "jailed about 280,000 people on political charges, and confined about 7,000 people in mental hospitals against their will." Although everyone knew of the existence of informants, few guessed there were over 160,000 of them. Until Lustration, that is. Lustration—"clarification through light and fire"—began in '92, right before I arrived, when informants' names were published in the newspaper. Over breakfast, Czechs learned which neighbor had been spying on them. Maybe someone they'd suspected. But maybe additionally a friend, lover, or relative. Understandably, Lustration did a number on my neighbors' eagerness to invite the new girl in 6B for *slivovice*.

After I'd returned to America in '94, my Czech year grew very distant very quickly. Květa and I exchanged Christmas cards. I used my manicure set. That was about it. I remained close with Kathleen, but she also returned to the States. I studied two other languages, which put Czech a few rotations back on the mental Rolodex. Sometimes I told the story—*Once, I lived in a place so polluted that dusk fell an hour earlier; once I was disliked by almost everyone I met.* But over time, that story became Mylar-wrapped, and I told it less.

Now I was reentering the story's setting, and gobsmacked to find it so changed. Prague had McDonald's and malls and cineplexes and internet cafés. I ate an arugula salad. I drank a fruit smoothie. I dined at an Indian vegetarian restaurant. I, too, had probably changed beyond recognition, at forty-two with three kids. Students didn't avoid me in the cafeteria—my eager poetry workshop students wanted nothing more than to go for a beer, ask me questions, laugh at my jokes. They invited me to Budapest over the long weekend, but I'd accepted Květa's invitation to stay with her and her husband, Petr. I can't say I was looking forward to it. Beyond the Christmas cards, we'd had no contact, and if things went badly I'd be trapped, without a car. But returning to Silesia felt like something I should do. It's healthy, I've always believed, to stay connected to one's past. It's healthy to unify one's selves. Doing so allows us to better understand who we are now.

As the train pulled into the station, I recognized Květa—her hippie hair had grayed but she was otherwise unchanged. I stepped onto the platform and we hugged, something we never did the year we shared an office. I gave Květa the bouquet I'd brought, and Petr carried my duffel to their car. They drove me to an outdoor beer garden. For old times' sake I ordered smažený sýr and ate the hell out of it while Květa took photos with her giant camera, and although I normally don't love a lens in my face, and certainly not while I'm yanking strings of melted cheese into my craw, I was bemused by her desire for documentation. I felt a palm on my shoulder and turned to find a smiling, elderly woman.

"We thought we'd never see you again," she said.

It was Hedvica. Květa, it turns out, had planned a reunion with my former colleagues.

"May I request a favor?" Hedvica asked, in her British-inflected, textbook English, after taking a seat. "Would you remove your sunglasses, so that I might better see your face?"

When I did, she smiled. "You quite look the same." She handed me notes from two former colleagues—Kristýna, caring for her "ailing mum," and Vlasta, with her new grandchild at their country *chata*. But the colleagues who were in town joined our table and began reminiscing, an unsettling experience in which I didn't recognize myself as the beloved character of whom they spoke.

"Don't you remember your nickname?" Květa asked.

"Sure I do," I sighed. I still hated it. "Američanka."

They laughed. "Oh yes, that's right."

I smiled painfully, waited for them to stop laughing, which took a minute.

"But don't you know your other nickname?"

Slowly, I shook my head.

"Ah," said Květa. "We called you 'Sunny Chicago.'"

Sunny Chicago? We were speaking English, but I felt lost. I wanted to whine, "Why didn't you call me Sunny Chicago in my hearing?" Such an affectionate nickname—Květa had never let on that she'd thought of me that way. But then again, she also had never let on how it must have rankled for me to waltz into her college with not a single day of teacher training under my belt, while she was teaching the languages of five countries she'd never been allowed to visit. I wanted to demand of her, "Why didn't you hug me while I wept about my dog?" But maybe, in that culture that afforded so little privacy, she thought the kindest thing she could do was exactly what she'd done, which was to ignore my sobs for a few minutes, then rise and leave, shutting the door behind her.

For half my life I'd thought of these people as antagonists, cast myself as the underdog. But that story seemed to have no recognizable features, no logical tie to the characters at this table, where sun rippled through the leaves and doused our group with an underwatery glow.

The waiter passed by and I asked him—Czech seemed to surface when I grasped, the Rolodex flipping forward—to tally the bill that's kept on the table. But it had already been whisked away. "You're too slow," he winked, then nodded at my colleagues.

Afterwards, Květa and Petr drove me to their house and showed me the guest room. The nightstand was cluttered with dozens of small wooden frames. Even from the doorway, I recognized the faces of my children, and my breath caught.

Květa gave an embarrassed laugh to see me so astonished. "I like to look at your Christmas cards. You have a beautiful family." She walked to a frame and straightened it. "I normally keep them in my bedroom, but I moved them here, because I thought you must be missing your children."

"Yes. Yes, I am," is all I could think of to say.

The next day Květa arranged outings to places I'd known two decades prior—"so you can stroll down memory lane." Wherever we went, I'd subtract the renovations and imagine myself into the scene. That outdoor market—minus the whitewash, minus the bright trays of strawberries and arugula, if given a sour, yeasty odor and a few bins of geriatric potatoes—might have been, yes, had been, the market I haunted, ordering in twos and fives.

The city's main square now resembled the square of any small European city. It had always been desolate, half the stores boarded up, but still a respite from the Brutalist architecture surrounding it. Now the buildings had been scrubbed of soot. The blue umbrellas of outdoor cafés shaded families eating gelato, gentlemen with newspapers and a coffee or a small beer. The fountain, formerly an empty shell, flung streamers of water that sparkled in the sun. There was, in fact, sun. Not once did I smell burning coal. A red flash was reflected in the pharmacy window—I swiveled my head to spy a spandexed runner. No one pointed. Though I wished to.

Sunday morning was to be the big outing, before I took the train back to Prague. First, we'd visit my old business college. I figured I'd look in on our old office, my classroom, and the mail room where I'd waited for letters from my (ex?) boyfriend that never arrived, an acceptance to graduate school that did. The cleaner-but-still-ugly building was locked, though, and Květa couldn't summon a guard. "Don't worry," I told her. "I'm more interested in seeing my old panelák."

After Květa photographed me in front of the college, we crossed the parking lot, feeling the July heat rise from the asphalt. I found the shortcut to my "estate." I set out with confidence on the dirt path and after a few turns spotted my building. But the grocery shouldn't have been so close. I moved down another row of identical buildings—*bingo*—but where were the dumpsters? Květa transferred her heavy camera bag to her other shoulder, revealing a bandolier of sweat, and Petr blotted his face. I turned left, and left again, then realized we were back where we'd started. Switching to Czech, Petr asked Květa if she needed to rest.

"I'm sorry," I said for maybe the fourth time.

"It's okay," she said, smiling, solicitous. "It's important that you find it."

Was it? I didn't know anymore. I felt confused, and guilty, and confused at feeling guilty. I didn't want to extend this sweaty parade. Yet I didn't want her to feel my comeback tour had been anticlimactic. I felt ashamed to reveal that I couldn't identify my panelák, that I no longer remembered my place in their world. That I had never understood it from the start.

What was one more misinterpretation, at this point?

"Here it is!" I cried, and pointed to a panelák. Květa raised her camera to her eye.

There I am—a very smiling, very trying girl.

That afternoon we said our goodbyes, and after another week in Prague I flew home to the arms of my beloveds. For the second time, I left that country a good bit less sure of myself and the world than when I'd arrived.

Closure: so satisfying. So tidy. But in this case, deceptively tidy. That Mylar-wrapped story, the one that begins, *Once I lived in a place so polluted that dusk fell an hour earlier; once I was disliked by almost everyone I met*—should I rewrite it, now that I've discovered the narrator was unreliable? Unsympathetic? Should I go about revising how lonely it felt to live there? If we're made up of the stories we tell about the stories we tell, who am I if a foundational story—a story I've used to motivate myself—has been mistranslated? How can one's selves be unified then?

The manicure set—the velvet case that springs open, the instruments in their elastic loops—I still use it.

I'd like Květa and the others to know that: I still use it.

But over the decades, some of the tools have disappeared, slipped from their elastic moorings. There's enough to work with, but when I use it now, I find myself wondering what else I've been missing all along.

Tree Pose

"Do not get attached to your thoughts," intones the yogi. "Observe without judgment." I stand on one leg, my right heel wedged high on my left inner thigh, my arms spread like branches. "Trees have no ego," she continues. I sense jittery movement off to both sides: the other trees flailing. Behind me, a clumsy tree falls. Not this tree: I root down. I pull sap to my leaves. Now the psychic yogi intones, "Stop comparing yourself to others. If you compare, you are not a tree, you cannot be a tree." Bitch, I'm a tree. I'm just a species of competitive tree.

Married Love: Missing Him

Come home from your trip, my tidy lover:

even the illicit pleasure of stacking my plate aslant in the washer
isn't a pleasure forever.

Character Witness

During the years in which I was writing my novel, the characters—the four main ones—became real to me, real people. Nevertheless, for reasons I've yet to fathom, the novel didn't sell and remains unpublished. Hence, the characters exist solely in the cramped quarters of my head. I feel bad about their confinement, but surely the characters themselves are at least partly to blame. They'd be free to take up space in the head of any reader they encountered, had they only behaved better, or, perhaps, worse.

Birthday

Even my earlobes look old.

Number One Sign You Shouldn't Send That Letter

Your tongue, dragging across the envelope glue, leaves a ghost of Malbec.

Dad Gave Us Twenty Dollars, Which Was a Lot in 1979

You were ten and I was eight during that vacation to Mackinac Island, you have to take a ferry across Lake Huron to get there, no cars allowed on the island, that's the whole point. You ride horse-drawn buggies everywhere. We stayed at the Grand Hotel, longest porch in the world if I recall, carpets patterned with geraniums I could still draw for you if I could draw, Mom bought plates in the gift shop, Mom was always buying plates in the gift shop. Everywhere the smell of fudge and horse droppings. There wasn't much to do after we'd strolled the porch and ridden a carriage, hence you begged Dad for money so we could hit the tourist drag, but even you didn't think he'd hand over—alongside the usual admonition to look after your little sister—a twenty. We strolled past the fudge shops, me deliberating: rocky road. No, peanut butter. No, rocky road. It was a big choice, I loved sweets, I was eight, I didn't often get to choose. You held the twenty, which made you even more the boss. That's when you pointed to a sign and announced, *Hey want to go to the House of Horrors, it'll be fun.* I squinted up at you, alarmed, resigned. You handed over the twenty and we were funneled into the entrance line, which wound through a dark red velvet one-way corridor, turning and narrowing, the dark passage growing darker, we could hear sounds coming from our future, whatever lay ahead of us, and whatever lay ahead of us was housing many horrors, I knew this in the bony fingers of my rib cage. Then through the wall I heard a woman scream. I whirled, began thrashing the wrong way through the dark tunnel, ramming bodies, big kids grunting in surprise, I was panting for my life, but the only one chasing me was you. Outside in bright sunshine, I could have wept with relief and maybe even did a little, collapsing on the curb, you bending over me, asking if I was okay but also pissed because I was such a baby, and even more pissed when you learned No Refunds: all of that beautiful twenty blown before we even got to the good part. Such a stupid stupid baby. I felt shame but knew I'd done what I had to do to survive, which is what you should have done that cold Chicago night, October 2008, almost thirty years later, you never should have gone in there alone, you never should have entered the dark red umbilicus, that narrowing tunnel, and when you realized the horror you were being funneled toward, you should have whirled and fled. When people recount their near-death experiences, they always say "I was walking toward the light" before some intervention—reminders of a loved one, some terrestrial duty left undone, etc.—recalled them, and then *presto* they were shuttled back to earth. Earthlings love these stories, warm their hands in that cozy "walking toward the light." I'm calling bullshit on that right now, my sister, bullshit, I say, bullshit, it was the dark that led you on, the light was behind you but you never looked back, the street, the sun, the fudge and horse droppings, your weeping baby sister, your stupid stupid baby sister, your duty on earth to look after her, to come outside and see if she's okay.

Two Sisters, One Fast, One Slow

It's impossible to say why I'm continually shocked that my sister didn't live to see forty.

I remember how she partied on her nineteenth birthday, her midlife crisis.

My Mother-in-Law in the Mirror

My mother-in-law was good.

I bet *that* sentence hasn't been written very often.

Betty Franklin was the kind of good one's tempted to call saintly. But we shouldn't call good people saints because that strips away their humanity—and responsibility for their actions. I'd wager she came out inclined toward goodness, but she was also good because she worked at it.

I'd known her for twenty years before I perceived that. Once, when the hall bathroom was occupied, I went into the one attached to her bedroom. On her mirror was a Post-it. "It's not about YOU," she admonished herself.

I've never seen a person less likely to think anything was about her, ever. She hated being the center of attention. Before I understood that, in our early days of dating, Tommy and I drove to Alabama to take her to lunch for her birthday, and I whispered the occasion to the waitress. In a moment the staff paraded over with a fat slice of cake, clapping and sing-shouting "Happy Birthday," forming a horseshoe around the table, urging her to blow out the candle. It was the cruelest thing I could have done to her.

She lived the quietest life imaginable. She liked to read the Bible in the early morning with her husband, holding hands. She liked to have dinner waiting for him when he came home from his mechanic shop. Her main activities were church and service work, bringing meals to elderly folks who couldn't get out or ferrying them to their doctor appointments. Otherwise, she liked to be home, where she managed the church's prayer chain, and managed to stay incredibly busy helping everyone who needed her. A homebody? Hoo boy. She lived an hour and a half from the Gulf of Mexico but never went to the beach. The only time she flew on an airplane was to attend our wedding in Chicago. Did she hate it? She didn't complain. But she went the rest of her life without replicating the experience. How hard she must have prayed to keep that plane aloft, borne on eagle's wings.

Her pleasures were simple; her greatest was being of use. Six of her eleven grandchildren lived next door, and two others close by (the remaining three, our own, were a six-hour drive away, an almost unthinkable distance for her, though the Franklins did make the drive a few times). "Can I fix you something?" she'd ask when a small body hurtled though her back door. Even in her late seventies, her own body failing, she'd ask that, ratcheting up her La-Z-Boy recliner and using the remote to change her Hallmark movie to *Blue's Clues*. She preferred serving others invisibly, without praise. She hated to be photographed, was embarrassed by gifts, distrusted compliments, dreaded clothes shopping, avoided all things fussy or expensive. She played the piano—when she was alone in the house. Her "beauty regimen" consisted of washing her face with Pond's cold cream. I never saw her drink a drop of alcohol. Married at age eighteen, she never had a job outside the home, never earned a single dollar. I never once heard her wish for anything advertised on television or mentioned by a neighbor. I never once heard her ask for anything besides photos of her grandchildren.

Maybe I'm so fascinated with Betty's goodness because we're opposites. Any Post-it stuck on my vanity mirror would proclaim, "Why YES, darling! It IS about you!" We're opposites in every way but the most important one—loving her son. Tommy grew up in Dickinson, Alabama—a country store and a cluster of houses surrounded by piney woods. His asthma was so bad as a boy that he couldn't sleep at night. He had to sit up in bed because lying down made the wheezing worse. Betty sat in a chair beside his bed every night, talking with him, sometimes reading him stories so he wouldn't feel scared when the breaths were difficult to pull into his lungs. So he wouldn't be alone with the owl-punctured dark. Tommy tells me they'd talk for hours, until finally Betty would say, "Hear that?" and he'd listen, and there it was, a log truck rumbling down the road. The log trucks started right before dawn, so this was always a welcome rumble, the signal that soon Tommy would be able to breathe. She'd kiss his forehead and he'd slide down a bit in bed and she'd say, "You can sleep now, sugar. You can sleep," and she'd return to her bed for her own few hours of slumber.

The world my husband grew up in could have embittered him. People treated like outcasts grow bitter. Tommy didn't want to hunt like the other boys, and he had no talent for fixing cars like his father and brother. What he wanted to do was write books and draw cartoons. Betty encouraged him, even as he moved out into a world that frightened her. He was the first person in his family to earn a college degree. And then an MA. And then an MFA, where we met, and where he wrote the first book he'd publish. A few years ago, one of his novels, *Crooked Letter, Crooked Letter,* was chosen as the English-language text that high school students in the south of Germany must study for their *Abitur*—their college entrance exam. I tagged along on his reading tour. The most surreal moment was in the famed lecture hall at the University of Heidelberg, where I stood in the back, admiring its grand proportions, its arched ceiling, its dark walnut walls covered by oil paintings and lit by sconces. This university, I'd read, was one of the world's oldest, chartered by Pope Urban VI in 1386, and has produced famous philosophers, writers, scientists, and twenty-nine Nobel laureates. Now it held a rapt, standing-room-only crowd listening to a first-gen college grad from a hamlet in Alabama read his story about his people. And I so swooned for Betty, whose pride would have equaled my own, that—though it sounds melodramatic—I had to steady myself on the chair in front of me.

When people talk about legacies, they usually mean buildings or civic projects or financial gifts. Betty's legacy is love. Her legacy is children who experienced it purely. Her legacy is the man I wed. Her legacy is my happy marriage.

She died of complications due to the Alzheimer's that developed in her last years, though I've always believed she commenced her dying on February 16, 2016, the day her husband of almost sixty years died. She took care of him from when he was in his twenties until he passed at eighty-two, and toward the end, when his health was in decline, his body failing part by part, that carework became full time. When he died, she lost her job.

I never heard her complain until the end of her life, when Alzheimer's started damaging her neural circuitry like rats nibbling the wiring in a house, invisible, insidious, the lights in her beautiful mind going out one by one. Before the diagnosis, but after we'd noticed worrying signs, we drove to her house to take her to a neurologist. We fetched lunch from Panera for all the grandkids, and Betty put her broccoli and cheddar soup in the fridge for later.

On the drive back from the tests, we heard her murmur something. "What, Mama?" Tommy asked. "I sure hope those kids don't eat my soup," she repeated. Tommy's eyes met mine in the rearview. We didn't need the neurologist to tell us she was sick. It was the meanest thing I'd heard her say in her entire life.

I lost a friend to cancer, and I used to think that was the worst death, to retain all of your faculties yet be unable to stop the body's vicious revolt. Yet now that I've seen a death from Alzheimer's, I'm not so sure. The slow, relentless, inexorable coring of someone's personality, the deletions of memories, experiences, words, thoughts; this may in fact be worse. At the end, she couldn't always recognize her children. There was so little left of her, but goodness remained. One of the last things she said to me was, "Can I fix you something?"

Hear that, Betty? It's the log trucks. You can sleep now, sugar. You can sleep.

Married Love: Double Dating

My husband and I decided that when it comes to other couples, it's ideal to like both halves of the couple evenly, 50% per spouse. And it's permissible, though not ideal, to like one spouse 60% and one spouse 40%. But liking one 100% and one 0%: such a couple is intolerable. 20%, we decided—20% is the lowest acceptable likability rating, even if the other spouse, scoring 80%, is quite delightful. It's important to have standards, we decided, this while dining alone because all of our couple friends were busy, though we'd made several calls. Yes, it's important to have standards, even though my husband and I, each an astonishing 100%, cannot possibly be held to them.

Prepping to Teach O'Connor While Visiting My Mother-in-Law

1. My mother-in-law has dementia, and my husband's mother-in-law also has dementia. My husband and I are married. What, I ask you, are the odds?
2. I've taught Flannery O'Connor's "Good Country People" a dozen times, but this time, sitting on my mother-in-law's couch, worried about my mother-in-law who tried to cut her chicken with the wrong end of her knife, the words don't penetrate. I skip over the story's intrigue and horror, straight to the fashion. How I'd love to be wearing, like Hulga, a "six-year-old skirt and a yellow sweat shirt with a faded cowboy on a horse embossed on it."

   I am the child here. That's what I'd like my clothing to broadcast. I am the child here. Me, me, me.
3. My husband's mother's favorite treat is giving her little dog his favorite treat. But because she has dementia, she forgets she's already given him his treat. Thus, the dog is fat. So fat that he can no longer jump onto the couch.

   During a recent visit, my husband noticed the dog had grown a strange ring around the base of his tail. We just knew it was a tumor. He took the dog to the vet.

   What's that? my husband asked, pointing at the tumor.

   That, said the vet, is fat.

   Fat?

   Yes, fat. Fat!
4. Over the last twenty-three years, my mother-in-law has also given me many, many treats.
5. Like Hulga, people with dementia see through to nothing. For

instance, the last time I visited my mother-in-law, I was in the living room when she shuffled out of her bedroom and lowered herself onto the other end of the couch. Before us, on the carpet, her fat dog lay beached. She gave it the side eye, glanced away, then whispered, stiffly, from the corner of her mouth, "I don't know what *that* thing is"—she jerked her head toward her dog—"but it's not good."

6. There are miracles that bring Christ and miracles that don't. Remember that dog so fat it couldn't jump onto the couch? When we're packing up to go, we find him on the couch.

   "How did you do that?" I ask, but he can't remember.

   The other miracle does not come to pass. She does not return to us. This is one of those days when she doesn't recognize her son. But this is the day we must leave. We must return home to care for my husband's mother-in-law, who also has dementia. Also, I'm teaching tomorrow. But what story? I can't remember. I've been reading it all morning, but I can't remember what story.

   I wonder if, later, I will pinpoint this moment as the onset of my early-onset dementia.

   We hug her goodbye. We carry our suitcases to the car, crushing evil-smelling wild onion under our feet. Another of her children arrives soon, I remind myself, but it feels like we're abandoning her. Without a crutch. Without a leg to stand on.

Two Sisters, One Slicing the Cake, One Choosing First

Keeping meticulous score was our favorite girlhood pastime.

Adjudicating the dispersal of the cereal box's plastic treasure.

Tallying who had more Christmas presents under the tree.

When given a piece of cake to split, one sister was handed the knife.
The other got to pick her half.

Quadruple fanatical eyeballs pressing down on the blade, its slow,
slow submergence through the buttercream.

And then (*poof*) you rolled over and played dead.

Took yourself right out of the game, fancy that.

So now I get everything when Mom dies. Everything! Where's the
fun in that?

Are you not rolling over in your grave?

Say *Uncle*, sister, I'll let you up.

I miss my mirror enemy.

Without you to sharpen myself against, I've lost my edge.

Being Sensitive About Being Sensitive

My husband and I are sensitive people, but we don't always share the same sensitivities.

Say we're dining out in our small town. My husband, who gets full easily, rarely finishes his entrée, which prompts the frowning waiter to ask, "Didn't you like it?" My husband doesn't want to offend the sensitivities of the waiter, whom we know, or the chef, whom we also know. So my husband asks for a to-go container, petitioning the waiter to assure the chef that the food was delicious, truly delicious, that he can't wait to eat it later.

Usually he does eat it later. But sometimes the food was not delicious. Sometimes he has no intention of eating it later. In these cases, he pitches the doggie bag as soon as we're out of sight, or parks it in our fridge until it gets tossed.

Which offends *my* sensitivities, because I'm sensitive to sea creatures. Plastic containers break down into microplastics, which wend their way to the sea. Will this container contribute to the bleaching of the coral reefs, reefs that can no longer provide nibbles for the parrotfish or shelter for the pygmy seahorse? Will its microplastics clog the bellies of humble crustaceans? I'm sensitive about the plastic clamshell encapsulating my husband's gelatinous seafood Alfredo. I'm sensitive about the clamshell because I'm sensitive to the clam.

It's easier when we're on vacation and my husband can assure the anonymous waiter that he loved his food but won't box it up because we're in a hotel room lacking a refrigerator. That's always a stroke of luck, lacking a refrigerator.

But here, in our small town, on date night, with our refrigerator nervously humming back at home, our intimate two-top gets quite crowded: on one side, there's my husband, the frowning waiter, and the offended chef; on the opposing side, there's me, the parrotfish, the pygmy seahorse, the humble crustacean, and the clam.

Strangers with Good Taste, That Is

That my family Christmas card has warped into a vanity project is now beyond dispute.

Throughout the year I'm constantly seeking the perfect family photo—all five of us in it, five pairs of open eyes, five smiling faces. Only when I'm certain I've identified such a photo can I relax for the year and design the card. I save time by printing address labels from a file on my computer, but even so the stuffing of the three hundred cards into the three hundred envelopes and the affixing of the three hundred stamps and three hundred address labels and three hundred return address labels requires a good chunk of November. I'm aware that, instead, I could simply post a photo on social media, but I enjoy the ritual, and content myself during the assembly by imagining the recipients gratefully sliding my family from the envelope, remarking on the fun we had in Sedona or Spain.

Further, such effort keeps us in touch with friends in other countries, friends who otherwise wouldn't see my children grow up.

Pat from Belgium is the most important of these friends. When I was fifteen, she lived with my family as a high school exchange student. Though we've only seen each other four times in the thirty-five years since she returned to Belgium, we've remained close. I've always believed my Christmas cards helped; thanks to my industry, she could witness my daughter bloom from awkward-in-braces to confident college junior, my middle child grow his hair long and find a swagger and a rock band, my "whoopsie" caboose enter the family and graduate from his stroller but remain the fêted family pet, his soft, squishy limbs the center of our scrum. Pat is loyal and loving and would cherish each card.

Yet one day last fall I received an echoey international phone call from Pat and her husband, Geert. Geert had a story to tell me. He'd had occasion to drive through their former neighborhood and discovered that their old house was having a yard sale. He pulled over to chat with the elderly couple who'd purchased their home sixteen years prior. When he approached, the wife inquired after his American friends.

"What American friends?" he asked.

"Your nice American friends," she answered. "You know, the ones from our Christmas cards?"

"What are you talking about?"

She detailed our appearance and yearly vacations.

Geert, recognizing my family, realized with shock that she'd received our card by mistake, and that she'd opened it and kept it, and that she'd continued to do so for the next fifteen years. He asked why she hadn't returned the cards, or forwarded them to the address that he knew, for a fact, she possessed.

"Because," she told Geert, "we've gotten such pleasure watching that nice American family grow up." She augmented his astonishment by disappearing into her house and returning with our most recent card, propped on her mantel since Christmas, though by this point it was October.

On the phone, we figured out that Pat had received the birthday cards I'd sent because I'd updated my address book, but I'd somehow neglected to update "Xmas Labels" on my computer.

"Sixteen years of cards!" shouted Pat, whom I'd never before heard angry. "I want to drive over to their house and tell them what I think!"

"Umm," I murmured.

"Can you believe how selfish that couple is?"

"Well . . ."

"How unbelievably selfish?"

Somehow I couldn't share her outrage, though I conceded it was a pity that the cards had been kept from her.

"People can be so crazy, right?"

"Yes," I said, laughing a little. "Crazy."

We ended the call on an off note. My dispassionate reaction had puzzled Pat and Geert, and subsequently puzzled me.

I understood my behavior only in December, upon nearly succumbing to the almost unbearable urge to send the homeowners a Christmas card. I'd like to suggest I was motivated by empathy for this couple who'd been following an engrossing serial for sixteen years, who'd had its story arc rudely interrupted. But I'm afraid the truth is uglier: the incident stoked my vanity. Your typical Christmas card merits admiration from friends. Finally, proof: Mine merits larceny by strangers.

My Sister Used to Give Me Blank Journals for My Birthday

My sister used to give me blank journals for my birthday, Christmas, whatever. In those years she was single, living in Wrigleyville, or she had one or another of her fun boyfriends. On summer weekends she'd go to street fests or art fairs, which Chicago seemed to host in giddy profusion, basically an excuse for day drinking while shopping and listening to bands. She knew I preferred unlined pages, less common at the stationer's, so she'd always make it her mission to buy me the prettiest blank journal, each a different height and heft, with covers of marbled paper or embossed leather or vintage fabric. She got a kick out of how much I loved them, her wordy, nerdy little sister. Gradually, because it takes a long time to fill a journal, I accrued a surplus. Each time I finished one, which was maybe every nine months, maybe longer, I'd carefully select another from my bookshelf. I must have amassed close to two dozen by the night my sister up and died without a word, as if she foresaw I'd never not need an empty room to howl in, for all the good it would do me.

Only the Basement

My sister believed that, as a girl, she'd been punished by being locked in the basement, in the dark.

We spoke of this only once. We were young adults, sharing a rare moment of unguarded intimacy. I could tell from the way she referred to being locked in the basement that she believed that I knew exactly what she was referring to, and that I, too, remembered it.

I didn't contradict her. But I have no memory of it. I would have been three, four, and five when she was five, six, and seven, the years in which she claimed our parents had sometimes locked her in the basement. Though I believe my sister believed it, I don't believe it, much.

Now my sister, who either was or was not locked in a dark basement, is dead. And my father, who either did or did not lock my sister in a dark basement, is dead. And my mother, who either did or did not lock my sister in a dark basement, has lost her memory. My mother, regarding remembrance, is as good as dead.

Now it's the truth that's locked in the basement. Only the basement knows it. Only the basement, and its confidant, the dark.

Flughafen Tempelhof

Say your husband gets invited to work in a château on a lake on the outskirts of Berlin. Say you're invited to accompany him: yes, four months have been granted you to work with your words.

Say it's autumn, 2016, season of the European migrant crisis, a crisis you knew little of before you came to Europe alongside—but in quite different circumstances than—1.3 million refugees fleeing their wars. Say you learn that many of them wind up in Germany because other countries don't want them, won't help them. Say Germany is chaos, but say Germany, at least, is trying. Say Berlin sets up a refugee camp in the most unlikely of places, a place straight out of a dystopian novel: an airport, abandoned eight years prior, marooned on the far side of the city, now housing seven thousand asylum seekers. Say you hear volunteers are needed to hand out donations. Say it's an eighty-minute bus ride from the château where you have four months to work with words, so what do you do—keep working and hate yourself a little, or stop working and hate yourself a little?

Say you ride the bus a long time through parts of the city you've never seen before and arrive at a chain-link fence beyond which squats in the distance—unlikely as a space station on Mars—an airport the Nazis built in the thirties. Say on the cracked runways hundreds of children in winter coats and hats are playing chase or flying kites.

Say you walk a long way across the tarmac and a long way through the airport (hallways lined with bunk beds, bedsheets serving as walls, you step over many legs, mostly male, mostly young), and find the volunteer center and are given many rules by the very German volunteer coordinator regarding how you will and will not clothe the refugees who line up behind the counter. Say you are taught to work without words, simply because there *are* no common words—some refugees are Syrians, some Somalis, some Afghans, Nigerians, Pakistanis and Ukrainians, Iraqis and Kosovars.

Say you are taught to talk through laminated cards. Say it goes like this: The refugee hands you a ticket, and you hand him a card with images of clothing. When he points to a coat, you show a card with pictures of small, medium, and large coats. Say he taps "large," so next you show the color card, on which he taps "black." Say this means you are to go into the storage room and choose two large black coats; he gets to select one. When you ask the very German volunteer coordinator what to do if he wants to keep both, she says, "He wouldn't dream of it." Say, to be fair, that she looks exhausted.

Say you do what you are told: take the ticket, show the card, come back with two of a thing, return the reject, take the next ticket.

Say you get used to doing all of this without words, so after a few shifts you shed words on the inside, too, because at some point you stop imagining their stories, stop picturing what tragedy finned after them as they rowed across the Aegean in a leaky boat, what terror snapped at their heels as they trudged over the Balkans in worn boots that you exchange for less-worn boots at a ticket counter at Flughafen Tempelhof, yes the very same airport that hosted the Berlin Airlift of 1948, when American and British planes broke the Soviet blockade and saved West Berlin by dropping supplies, coal and milk and flour and medicine, even chocolate bars for children tied to handkerchief parachutes, called "Operation Little Vittles."

Say by shift's end you aren't thinking about saving anyone but yourself because your back hurts, you stomp your boots in the snow as you wait for the 10 p.m. express bus, you don't remember falling asleep but you wake when your forehead knocks the greasy window, the airport funk clinging to your hair; say you don't feel particularly noble; it's important to say this, you don't enjoy this work and you don't feel noble doing it, but you return, you keep returning, keep standing behind the counter, keep taking the tickets, showing the card, the card, the card, because, in a way you're ashamed of, you hope this weekly labor buys you six guiltless days in the charming château where you have come to use your words.

Say you're scheduled to leave Germany and on your last shift, which is almost over—the counter closes at 9:30 p.m. and it's 9:30 p.m., thank God—the line ends with a mother and her daughter. Say the mother is young, pretty, despite a half-grown-out platinum dye job and too much makeup in the harsh airport fluorescents. Say the daughter is pretty or say she is beyond pretty or say nothing at all because words are a valueless currency in a flightless airport. Say her dark ringlets cascade down her narrow shoulders and her eyes are large and blue and clear from being scrubbed by wars, by all she has seen in her—what—six years?

Say she points to a picture of a coat. Say you bring two coats. Say she hardly studies them before she shakes her head, her curls tossing. Say you look down at the coats and are surprised to find you agree, they will not do. Not for her. Say you return to storage and choose two more, an action likely verboten by the very German volunteer coordinator. Say you select these two with care, when you slide them across the counter you are almost proud. Say she huffs and shakes her head again. Say you glance at the mother, who glances away; this girl and her caprices are your problem now.

Say you return a third time to storage and head for the rack you've been told to ignore, the problem rack. Say you feel it before you see it: fur, maybe rabbit; it's a zip-up rabbit jacket tailored for a six-year-old, okay sure a little bald at the seams, but basically a miracle, a miracle jacket, and you bear it in your arms and slide it under her gaze, her long eyelashes throwing shadows on her cheeks as she works the teeth of the zipper, checks the pocket linings, and finally tries it on—something no other client has done—unsmilingly zips it to her chin and revolves, an ice princess on top of a sled speeding away from here, speeding through the woods tugged by horses running fast, horses racing the snowflakes that land gently on the tips of her rabbit fur and sparkle in the moonlight.

Say your bus is leaving, the express that, if missed, delays your arrival at the château by thirty minutes. Say that just when you know she'll accept the jacket and you'll jog for your bus—just then your princess produces another ticket. Say she taps "pants," taps "blue," and rejects the jeans you bring because, like all donated German jeans, they are eighties jeans or nineties jeans, they are wide-leg jeans and she doesn't want wide-leg jeans, she wants skinny jeans, it's 2016 and she wants 2016 jeans, which means skinny jeans, don't you get it, skinny—she tells you this without words and you satisfy her without words while the mother wanders off with a pack of cigarettes.

Say the girl, still wearing the fur jacket, skinny jeans flipped over her arm, produces one last ticket and points to the accessories card, first to a backpack and next to a stuffed animal. Say you reenter the storage, scanning the shelves for the pink glittery backpack you spotted weeks ago, but it could be anywhere now, pink glittery backpacks don't linger at the repurposed airport's repurposed lost luggage, but your task on earth is to find it, your express bus has expressed itself away and you will satisfy her if you have to walk back to the château, if you have to crawl on your knees, yes you will present her with the backpack that will earn you a smile.

Say you find the miracle backpack and then jackpot upon a two-eyed teddy bear in this land of one-eyed teddy bears. Say you slide them over the counter and she examines both and then, without smiling, pulls the backpack close. Say you reach for the bear, already turning away, already girding yourself for the slushy trudge to the bus stop, when the bear is snatched clean out of your grasp. Say you're startled, and later you'll wonder if it's that, being so startled, that makes your training kick in. You whirl to face her, you tap her single ticket on the counter and then raise your finger in the air to remind her she must choose one. Say that she, without unzipping her blue gaze from your gaze, unzips the backpack, stuffs the bear inside, zips it up, then thrusts her finger at your face: *one*.

Say she does smile then, but in contempt.

One, her finger thrusts again, and then she threads her arms through the straps of the glittery backpack, settles it over her balding rabbit jacket, and saunters away down the terminal.

Say her contempt is the blessing, the boon of your *Ich bin ein Berliner* phase, say her contempt is the reason she alone of the crowd, the host of seven thousand, is lodged in the abandoned airport of your memory, say this is because, you imagine, it's her contempt that has offered her asylum; it's her contempt that has warmed her with fur and armed her with teeth, her contempt that she has clutched on a strange cot at night and her contempt that has clutched her in return, her contempt that she has threaded her arms through and toted with her everywhere. Say she is alive—*say it, with words*—alive you imagine her, yes you imagine her, alive because she nurtures such an exquisite contempt for death, and her contempt has catapulted her out into the moonlit snow where even now she is whipping the horses to make them run faster, whipping the horses unnecessarily, whipping the horses simply because she can.

Me vs. Slugs: Pandemic Edition

When the terrible virus was unleashed and our lives screeched to a halt, I planted a vegetable garden. My first. I tended it zealously, with the darting eyes of a suicide bomber. This was March, April, May, the world hijacked by hysteria. I could have watered my garden with my tears after returning from the store rumored to have toilet paper, after scrubbing my hands and changing my clothes and scrubbing my hands and disinfecting every sack of off-brand rice, every dented can of beans.

So, the garden. I would grow our groceries. I would knit a chlorophyll blanket to keep my family snug and safe.

At first, it worked. Everything grows in Mississippi, even for a "gardener" googling "how to plant a seed." In a Mississippi minute, sprouts were sprouting: #winning.

Until the day my frothy cilantro fronds went missing; only their naked flagpoles remained, resembling chives. The next day, no poles. And, for that matter, no chives. My fennel (yes, I'd grown it solely for the name) was depilated. My dill, deadheaded. What invisible blight was this? My garden was syruped in sunshine, watered daily, and mulched to keep my sproutlings moist.

Slugs, said Google. Slugs shimmy from under the mulch at night. They munch until dawn, then slime back under the mulch, engage in some hermaphroditic kink, then squirt out thirty eggs. And you know what happens to the eggs. Everything grows in Mississippi.

Beer, said Google, a plate of beer is the answer. I poured a can into a Frisbee, placed the shallow grave in the garden, set my alarm for 4:30 a.m. With my phone flashlight I returned. Six or seven gray bloated bodies lolled in their Bud Light Jacuzzi. But angling my phone, I could see other slugs still chomping. Not thirty, but thirty times thirty times thirty, the flagstones glistening with their calligraphy, the screen door snotty with secretions. I donned my gardening gloves like a knight would his gauntlets, plucked a fat slug from a leaf of butter crunch, and chucked it into the grass. But it was probably already U-turning to resume its salad course. I plucked another, gritted my molars, and squished. Enough: I didn't have the stomach for it.

Two-thirds of my children accepted the bribe, a dime a slug, thrilled to be out past bedtime and armed with flashlights. The nine-year-old earned $2.60, the fourteen-year-old $4.10. But the next night they quit after only a buck apiece. "There aren't any more," they claimed the third night. But, oh, the slugs were there. I could feel them crawling in the tender hollow at the back of my neck.

I foraged deeper into Google, which now said beer was not the answer; instead, wait for midnight, make a pail of suds, drop the slugs in. They'd die beneath the bubbles, and I wouldn't have to watch or assist.

Google was right about the soapy water, but beer was still the answer. I drank it steadily, girding for battle. Then I rampaged through my garden until every last slug had been dunked. The next day, I made my husband empty the sluggish pail. Game over.

Months later, when things were still bad but better, when we understood how the virus spread, and learned to wear masks, and thought we might survive, my fourteen-year-old mentioned the night of my slugfest, mentioned hearing me in the garden.

"Oh really?" I asked uneasily.

"Yeah," he said. "I woke up, and I could hear you cursing."

"Cursing?"

"Yeah."

It remains to be seen how historians will contextualize this long dark pall of pandemic, the fraying of global mental health, the toll on our children's futures. And that official reckoning will overlap with our private reckonings, the large suffering as well as the smaller stories, the cringeworthy, told for a laugh. Perhaps at a dinner party, say, people offering up their personal pandemic low. I won't have to scramble for mine. That night, which should have rightfully slipped into oblivion, is now freshly imagined from the point of view of my son, lying in his bed, in the dark, listening to his drunkish mother marauding in the Mississippi night.

"You kept calling them"—he broke off—"Can I say the word? Without getting in trouble?"

I nodded.

"—assholes. You'd shout at each slug, before dropping it in the pail, 'You're a little asshole.'"

I closed my eyes in a slow blink.

"And—" he continued.

"Yeah?"

"Sometimes you'd laugh."

This Little Trick I Play on Myself

When I fantasize about being single, and being childless, and living in a modern apartment in a European capital, I remind myself that if that *were* my life, I'd fantasize about being married, and having children, and living in a comfortable home in a small town, which *is* my life.

My imagined me provides a useful elixir.
Revived by her envy, I rise to make dinner.

Married Love: Rolf und Helga

When we arrived at the château for the writing residency, we found everything delightful, from the gracious, well-appointed rooms to the manicured grounds abutting the lake. Even the lawnmowers were delightful. There were two of them, robotic mowers—we'd never seen such a thing—silently gliding across the green, pivoting when nearing fence or forest, sentient as the planchette of a Ouija board. We fancied that we could tell them apart, granted them names and personalities. Before long, we were crafting their witty dialogues, cracking ourselves up, relishing our quirky marital humor.

Later in the residency we learned that everyone, absolutely everyone, who stays in the château is charmed by the mowers. One night in the château's library we even came across a well-known writer's well-published account of staying in the château, mentioning the mowers. We recognized the satisfaction she took in whimsically assigning the mowers names (the wrong names).

We still found the château delightful, but less so.

The Hug

Your musician friend was dear to you. You were dear to each other. You instigated his move to your town, in fact. The day you met, one glorious July afternoon on Martha's Vineyard, he told you he loved North Mississippi hill country blues and had always wanted to check out the area. You made a good case for him to visit. When he did, he decided he'd found his home.

Ever since, you'd met frequently for drinks or dinner, sometimes just the two of you, sometimes with your husband and your friend's newest plus-one. Often you'd watch his band play, and you'd always end up dancing, and you could tell he liked that. His shows would go late, though, too late for you on school nights, so you'd slip out before the end. As you did, you'd see a little puff of air leak out of him, see his bravado wobble. Truth is, he was secretly sweet on you, but you never discussed it—you didn't need to. You both understood that in a parallel universe where you were single and he wasn't so much older, you'd have dated. Instead you were just good friends, a situation that worked fine for happily married you, but maybe a bit less fine for him, which is why you always felt a smidge guilty when he confessed to being lonely. You tried setting him up with your most fabulous single friends, but it never took. Maybe if it had, you'd have felt jealous. It's flattering, after all, being the object of someone's regard.

One night you drank margaritas at a Mexican restaurant and he rehashed his latest breakup and you gave him a pep talk and you ended the night laughing, making plans for your group of friends to visit Napa Valley, a place he knew well. He walked you to your car and you hugged goodbye. This time, though, he didn't release you after the usual quick squeeze. The hug kept hugging. The hug wasn't creepy, he didn't go in for a kiss, his hands stayed high on your back, but suddenly you became aware that in a tight hug you're basically pressing your breasts against the other person's chest. How have you never noticed that before? Maybe because, in a hug of normal duration, you don't have time to identify body parts. In this hug, you had time—yep, those are your tits mashing his chest, all right—and just when you felt a distinct need to free yourself and tensed a bit, he dropped his arms, so everything was okay, and you didn't need to discuss it.

Within months, he'd be dead. A stroke.

The earth keeps turning, sure, and you still love music and you still go to shows, but when you look up, nobody's watching. Nobody smiles when you dance. Nobody sighs when you leave.

Pathetic, how badly you could use a hug.

Lullaby

My sister worked with abused children, helping them navigate the court system and foster care. It was a tough job, and she was a tough broad, as tough as the Chicago neighborhood where she lived with her boyfriend. On one side of their apartment building, a busy fire station, loud with sirens and roaring engines. On the other side, a busy Vietnamese church. On Sunday mornings, she'd leave threatening notes under the wipers of any churchgoers who dared to park in her spot.

When I moved to Arkansas, my sister and her boyfriend came to visit. That first morning, over coffee, she said it took her forever to fall asleep: *Too goddamn quiet here*. Finally her boyfriend had gotten the idea to sing to her to sleep. *What song?* I asked, charmed. He'd toggled the two notes of a siren in her ear.

Fennessy

A successful writer friend publishes a new novel. My husband and I always read his novels, and this will be no exception.

My husband reads it first. When he finishes, he sits me down. He wants me to know before I read it: our writer friend has kinda sorta used my sister's name. He's used her first name, and he's used her nickname, and for her last name he's changed one double letter into a different double letter.

"The character isn't based on your sister, though," my husband says. "Everything besides her name is different."

I take this in. "Why would he do that, do you think?"

My husband lifts a shoulder, speculates, "He must have just needed a very Irish-sounding name."

I nod. Our writer friend is a good guy. When my sister died, he sent me a Tiffany picture frame—to hold a photo of my sister, he wrote in the sympathy card.

"Should I not read the novel?" I ask my husband.

"I think it's okay," he says. "I think you can handle it. But I wanted you to be prepared. It's a bit of a shock, you know. Seeing the name."

Thus forewarned, I'm able to read and even enjoy the novel. It's true what my husband said. The character is not my sister. The character is murdered in the first chapter. The rest of the novel is the main character trying to figure it out. My sister was not murdered, and in the novel of my life, her death would occur maybe in chapter five or so. Though it's true that the rest of the novel would still be the main character trying to figure it out.

It's also true what my husband said about the name being a

shock. Every time it strikes my eyes, I read my sister's name, autocorrecting. The double *s* yanked into double *l*, shoelaces pulled taut.

In this way, reading the novel *is* like reading my life. The main character keeps tripping over the minor character, who exited early.

Who gets to decide who is main and who is minor? Who gets to decide who exits early? Some joker who seemed like a good guy. Some joker gets to decide who ends up framed, who turns the page.

While You Were Out

I birthed a son, and he is ten, imagine that, you missed ten birthdays of your nephew, you who gave the most expensive, least practical gifts, the gifts that were age-inappropriate, too loud, too many pieces, choking hazards—you know, the gifts my children loved best. The older children, that is. Which proves just how long you've been out: after the children you spoiled, there came a third, a baby, but the baby's no longer a baby, in fact there's only one secret cache of baby left. The undercrease where chin meets neck. I could show you, but sister you must hurry. It smells like his stuffed monkey and glue sticks and earthworms and maple syrup, it smells like God. You would undie to snug your nose there, you would be justified returning from the box they stashed you in, like that ghost story we whispered at sleepaway camp, the girl buried alive, when her coffin was finally opened, ten clawed-off fingernails lodged in the wood like Lee press-ons. I'm sorry to be stupid in the middle of this memo, but is it really possible I had a child while you were out? A child who's ten? Sometimes the longer you know a fact the more unreasonable it seems. If I could take a sheet from this pink pad, fill out the "message" box, then place this memo on your desk, this is what I'd write: Three years ago in church the no-longer-baby began to squirm. Intuition bade me turn. He held my gaze, squaring his little shoulders in his little khaki suit, then reached into his chest pocket and teased out a twenty-dollar bill, a bill I *knew* he hadn't owned before the basket heaped with offerings had made its slow pass down the pew. What did he do then, O my sister? He grinned. A shit-eating grin if you want to know, seven years old and missing a front tooth, the other glinting in the churchlight. How can you resist a little devil like that, I ask you. No, really. I'm asking you. Cease resisting, while there's still chinsweet to be slurped. Delay no more, because puberty, etc. And here's a further inducement: how long it's been since your last cigarette! You must be jonesing so bad, jonesing for a Marlboro, which you sometimes called your *smoky treat*, sometimes called your *coffin nail*. Picture that first drag, how sweet that tar would taste. Remember your dazzling French inhale? All the pretty vices could be yours again! So: enough. I've marked this memo *Urgent*. I've checked the box *Wants to see you*. Make it happen. I believe. I am the faithful. I carry a coffin of matches always, for when your cigarette needs a light.

The Irish Goodbye

How, without farewells, you slipped out the back door of the party of your life, O my sister.

A Scrap of Paper That Says *Remember*

"I'd like to come visit," my mother said, calling from her home in Illinois, early March. "For St. Patrick's Day."

"Mom," I said, from my home in Mississippi, "you can't. I'm sorry, but you can't. This new virus, Corona? It's serious. And it's killing people, particularly elderly—"

"Who are you calling *elderly?*"

Earlier that year, she'd asked me not to throw her a big birthday party, as I'd done for her seventieth and seventy-fifth. She'd decided to ignore turning eighty. She's beautiful, my mother, and passes for younger. She has a patrician air, and green eyes with small pupils that are coolly penetrating, used with sobering effect on my high school boyfriends.

But there was no ignoring her increasing memory loss, at least for me. She was repeating herself at times, struggling for words at others. Further, the last time she drove me in her wide sedan, it drifted from lane to lane like a party barge. She was blithe to the angry beeps from passing motorists, while I flinched and stomped my imaginary brake pedal. I screwed up the courage to ask her to pull over. After we traded places, I faced her and articulated the sentence I'd practiced and dreaded: "Mom, you shouldn't be driving anymore."

She waved her fingers, as if to say "To each his own."

I inhaled. "And you should be tested for Alzheimer's."

"I *have* been tested," she said. "I don't have Alzheimer's."

"Can I talk to your doctor?"

"He's busy."

She changed the subject, in the same way she'd done when my husband and I suggested she move to Mississippi. She hated change, she liked her home, her friends, her church. But I worried about her living alone, my father long dead, my sister now, too. If something happened to her, how would I take care of her from so far away?

And now something *had* happened. A global pandemic. She was the only player who showed up for bridge, and called me to complain.

"But, Mom," I said, "the others probably didn't go because it's *not safe*. You shouldn't be cruising for bridge partners, either. You shouldn't be touching cards and passing them, you shouldn't be sitting knee-to-knee at a small table."

She sniffed, unconvinced.

So, no more bridge. Or book club. St. Mary's closed its doors, which meant no more mass, no more post-mass coffee with "the girls." Then the community center shuttered, so no more tai chi or aqua aerobics. No movie theaters. Of course, the same closures were curtailing our lives in Mississippi, but shelter-in-place feels different when your shelter hums with four other humans. And, sad as I was that our oldest had been sent home from her first year at college, I luxuriated in gathering my babies around my table, no one begging to dine out with friends or rushing off to band practice.

For my mother, isolated, each canceled activity was a door shutting to the world beyond herself. To the neurons that would have fired when she was counting bridge tricks or practicing her Golden Rooster in tai chi.

And now she was asking to visit for Easter.

"Mom . . ." I faltered. I was raised in a strict Irish Catholic family, in a stately Victorian home—Victorian inside as well as out. *If you don't have anything nice to say, don't say anything at all* was a constant refrain. *Children should be seen and not heard* was another. My sister and I were taught to be obedient and uncomplaining, no matter the circumstances. She rebelled, but I internalized those lessons so thoroughly that it took me decades to unlearn them, to speak out when speaking out was called for. My life in Mississippi bears little resemblance to my upbringing in Illinois. Our three children are loud and messy and confident. And I've grown into a confident adult. But it still pains me to displease my mother.

"Mom, it's too risky. If the kids gave you the virus . . . . But this can't go on forever. When we have a vaccine. . . ."

In addition to being terrifying, Covid has been tedious, everyone trading the same grievances, always ending with the wish for a vaccine, so life can "return to normal." But my mom was lonely, and likely depressed, and her decline was accelerating. A vaccine might stop Covid but couldn't reverse Covid's damage. That land called "normal"? Already I knew not all of us would be returning there.

I doubled down, sent little gifts, cards from my kids. We spoke daily, and when we did, Mom repeated herself, called me by her sister's name. I tried to teach her how to use Zoom so she could watch mass or join her friends for happy hour, but the computer baffled her. One day, I called in time to stop her from sending money to an internet scammer. Another day, she locked herself out, and later when I reached her on the phone, she told me the locksmith was her first face-to-face conversation in months. "Face-to-face?" I asked. "You mean mask-to-mask? You wore masks, right?"

"Oh, probably," she said, "but don't worry, he was a very nice young man."

I explained, again, how the virus is passed, face-to-face, even by very nice young men. I asked her how much the locksmith charged. She didn't remember. She paid him cash.

This couldn't continue. My husband wondered if we should just pile the kids into our minivan and drive the eleven hours to spring

Nana from her solitary confinement. We might kill her with Covid. But protecting her from it was also killing her.

We were discussing our options when my mother called. "Beth Ann," said this woman famous for her stiff upper lip, "you need to come home. I'm falling apart."

I flew to O'Hare, coating myself with mucusy Purell, and took a car service to my mother's house. I hurried up her walk—this was the longest I'd gone without seeing her. She opened the door and I hugged her, the hug I had been anticipating for months. But it felt wrong, all wrong. She was small in my arms. Her sweater was stained. Her house had an odor. She tried to ask about my flight. But she wasn't fumbling for an occasional phrase; she struggled to finish a sentence, each word a fish slipping out of her hands. My beautiful mother, her green eyes not piercing now, but pierced.

She led me to the kitchen, mumbling vaguely about dinner, but the weird lumps of food she pulled from the fridge didn't look or smell fresh.

"Mom," I said, "rest. I'll go pick something up." She began to protest as I walked toward the door leading to her garage, but I kept going, saying, "I'll borrow your car and be back in a minute."

She was still protesting when I opened the door and drew up short. Her car's front was smashed like a tin can. Now she was behind my shoulder, cringing at being discovered, like the teen I'd been, busted for sneaking in past curfew with a fresh dent in the station wagon. I'd heard about this, your parent becoming your child. The transference was complete.

After that, things moved quickly. She agreed to let me call her doctor. Who said that he'd often asked for permission to speak to me, but she'd assured him I was "too busy." Dr. Nguyen agreed Mom shouldn't live alone. She needed full-time care. My mom had been truthful at least about not having Alzheimer's; her diagnosis, "mild cognitive impairment," is similar, however, and similarly degenerative, and likely to pair with Alzheimer's.

Two weeks later, my husband and I flew back to pack up her house, no small task, stuffed as it was with antiques she'd inherited and collections she'd amassed over decades. While winnowing the furnishings of her house to fit a one-bedroom assisted living, I kept finding tiny scraps of paper, notes she'd written to jog her memory. Most of them had to do with me. "Poet laureate," read a tiny curl of paper by her desk phone. "Poet loreit," read another by her kitchen phone. I'm the poet laureate of Mississippi, a fact she's proud of, and, I suppose, wanted to get right when boasting to friends or frenemies. Other scraps held the name of the literary festival I'm organizing. "Ask Beth Ann," read another. I tucked one scrap into my wallet; it said, simply, "Remember."

Mild cognitive impairment can't be reversed, but it can be slowed. That's what we hope is happening now, in her new life, not even one mile from our house. Even here, Covid is managing to put the screws on—Mom isn't allowed to leave the grounds of her assisted living, which means she can't come to our house, not even for Sunday dinner. But after her first seventy-two hours of in-room quarantine, we've been allowed to visit. She has to stay inside the building, and we sit outside, masked, at the end of a six-foot table. Until yesterday, we'd had to speak with a glass door between us, using intercoms, like a bad prison movie. ("What are you in for?" I wanted to joke, but she doesn't get jokes anymore.)

Yesterday, finally, the glass door was opened. I'd brought my nine-year-old and a late summer plum cake, which I bake every September when the plums are ripe and sweet. We'd brought the cake, still cinnamon-warm, so she could share with the other residents hanging out by the hummingbird feeders. I want her to make friends. And cake makes friends.

She's been out of quarantine for a week, and yesterday seemed a bit more herself, especially when directing her grandson to the residents deserving of plum cake. "Him?" I indicated a long-legged man cruising by on a motorized scooter with a flapping flag. "Not *him*," Mom said. "He's *loud*." Then she instructed, "Make sure Richard gets some." Hmm, I thought. Mom has a friend, and she remembers his name.

When the nurse came to tell us our hour was over, I slid the last piece of cake across the long table to Mom and stood, my arms awkward at my sides when they yearned to hug her.

The nurse asked my mom, "Do you want me to carry your cake to your room?"

"Fat chance!" she said. "I'll keep it in my protection."

And I swiveled my head to marvel at her teasing tone and easy sentence.

I'll never know what my mother's mental state would have been if she hadn't suffered six months of isolation. I'll never know what Covid took from her. But it didn't take everything. And it did bring her close, right down the street, while there's still a lot of sweetness to enjoy.

Late summer plum cake.

Remember.

Married Love: Twenty-Fifth Anniversary

When, to present me a ring, he drops to one knee, it cracks.

It Is Hard When Your Job Is Hard but Doesn't Appear to Be So

For instance, when the lawn crew arrives and you are reading. You are aware of how this looks. You are aware that if they glance through the window, they will see a woman in her pajamas reclining in an easy chair, reading. They cradle heavy leaf blowers, wear goggles and earplugs. Your slippered feet are propped on an ottoman. They are well within their rights to think, Look at that idle woman. But in fact your reading—student papers, student poems, dense literary criticism—is far from easy, though you read in an easy chair. Sometimes, in order to keep from quitting, you must bully or cajole yourself. You are fatigued from this reading, though it doesn't show, so you get no credit for your stamina. If only, when reading difficult material, your face grew red and sweaty. If only your breathing grew ragged and labored. Like during great exertion at the gym. Dead Lift and Chest Press. Hammer Curl and Lat Raise. And now, the hardest exercise of all: Lick Finger to Turn Page. You can do it, B.A.: two more sets of eight reps.

The Trespass

1.

She's picking daffodils in an abandoned lot, stepping among the tall grasses. As she gathers her bouquet, she narrates her actions in third person, a habit retained from a girlhood spent in books, an odd amusement. She's not supposed to be here—the driveway is cordoned off with a NO TRESPASSING sign—but this lot has sat untouched in the twenty years she's lived down the street. The daffodils, which grow in large swaths around what must have been a grand house—now just a brick chimney—can't be seen from the road, due to the overgrown driveway, and the lot is backed by deep woods. So she gathers all she can, reasoning that if *she* were a daffodil, she would rather be picked and arranged in a vase than left to shrivel unadmired.

When she hears a crashing sound in the woods behind her, she jolts upright, dropping her armload of flowers.

Now her narration draws up short. It began as nonfiction, realistic nonfiction, but, she suddenly sees, it's fairy tale adjacent. Here, at the fringe of the woods, that liminal space, enough conventions of the fairy tale have been met to trespass genres.

She stoops to gather the flowers, pondering the likelihood of her success as a fairy tale protagonist. Condensed answer: not bloody likely. Hasn't she been a little smug, relishing her secret stash of daffodils? And blithe as well, turning her back to the dark woods as she pilfers this gold? Further, hasn't she been greedy? After all, she grows daffodils in her own garden; she could pick those for a bouquet, but she enjoys regarding them from her window. And then there's her biggest sin of all: she's wearing a cute little polka-dot dress. It's not merely that a bad thing *might* happen to her.

It's that a bad thing *must* happen, and when it does, everyone will feel vindicated.

How can she save herself? Think, Beth Ann!

Suddenly she sees her ticket out: her mother! She's picking these daffodils for her mother! Her mother is elderly, in a home for the elderly: these daffodils will smear their buttery joy around that otherwise dreary facility. And, ahhh, a different fate entirely awaits a character risking so much danger to cheer her ailing mother.

Phew. That was a close one. The dutiful daughter continues picking daffodils.

2.

She doesn't give her mother the daffodils. They look too good on her mantel.

3.

That night a sinkhole yawns open underneath her house and it sucks her house down and collapses it around her and she smothers, using her last breath to scream. The end.

A Woman's Head Is Not the Safest Place to Be

All it takes is a dark entry, how we must turn our vulnerable backs to the night to unlock the tricky door, the key not quite catching, jiggle jiggle—for women to hear footsteps. We know what's next: the blow to the head, the white paneled van. Most men would never guess how often women are raped and murdered in their heads. A woman's head is not the safest place to be. Even here, in this Swiss village, this stupidly beautiful Alpine Swiss village ringed by wheat fields stretching to Lake Geneva. Even here, when I'm out for a run on the dirt path between farms, all it takes is a large man stepping out of the wheat at the crest of the hill and striding toward me for it to begin. He will knock me into the hip-high waving wheat where my struggle will be disguised as more waving, he will gag me with golden tassels, he will wrap my braid around his fist and bang my skull into baked earth. As the distance between us is halved, I wonder if he will cart my corpse away or leave it for the vultures, and I've nothing to drop to alert the dogs other than my wedding ring, and if I'm to be raped and murdered I want my wedding ring, it gets inside your head, our culture gets inside your head and makes you first rape yourself, then murder yourself, then blame yourself after, when what the nice Swiss farmer says in passing is *Bonjour.*

Elegy

FOR ROBERT HELLENGA

1999. I was the English Department's new hire. He'd been teaching there for decades. One night at a party, deep in our cups, we discovered a shared passion for Yeats, ended up outside under blooming wisteria, chanting, "Like a long-legged fly upon the stream / His mind moves upon silence."

"When I die," he said, "I want you to recite 'The Long-Legged Fly' at my funeral."

"Sure thing," I said.

"I'm serious," he said. "At my funeral, I want you to recite 'The Long-Legged Fly.'"

"You bet."

"You mean it?"

"Absolutely."

"Promise?"

"I promise."

After teaching in that prairie town for two years, I moved south, nine hours south. But I thought of that promise intermittently. I wondered if he, too, thought of it, and if he expected me to honor it. Surely not. Although we enjoyed each other and exchanged a few letters over the years, we never saw each other again. First, five years had gone by, then ten, then fifteen. And in each one of those years, my life grew increasingly crowded with the needs of others, my carework a shawl I never stopped knitting but could never spread far enough to cover all who needed shelter. As a result, I grew canny, I had to, canny about expenditures of energy. I practiced hesitating before agreeing to favors, practiced asking myself sobering questions, questions such as *Who in their right mind would drive nine hours to honor a twenty-year-old, whiskey-soaked promise?*

Thus seasoned, when he died, I kept my head down. I stayed the course.

But I'm haunted: not by my former colleague, and not by Yeats or his long-legged fly, but by the ghost of the girl I'd once been. A girl who'd vault from her right mind in an instant for something essential, like making good on a lavish promise.

Dearly beloved, this is her elegy.

Related Searches

When a user searches in Google, the results page suggests other commonly searched terms.

For example, if you search my name, related searches include:

Beth Ann Fennelly **micro-memoirs**
Beth Ann Fennelly **poems**
Beth Ann Fennelly **ted talk**
Beth Ann Fennelly **biography**
Beth Ann Fennelly **sister**

The first time I saw this last related search, I was shocked. Shocked, but not for long.

When I thought about it, searching for my sister made a lot of sense. After all, I'm also searching for my sister, though in a different way, of course. The reader, I assume, is simply searching for the manner of her death.

I haven't been consciously withholding this information from the reader—I haven't been consciously withholding anything from anyone besides myself—but I see now that this narrative gap could frustrate. I've written so much about grieving my sister, but I haven't said what happened. What happened, it's safe to say, has not been made available to users. Thus, users have fled into the many-armed embrace of Google.

In high school, just so you know, I was accused of being a tease.

The lesson seemed to be that if you make someone desire something, you'd better be prepared to hand it over.

You'd think I'd have learned my lesson. You'd think I'd have learned my lesson, and written it down, so we could quit searching.

Because My Editor Suggests I Reveal How My Sister Died

I write, You're right. The absence calls attention to itself

I write, Reader, I'm not trying to be coy. Which is true—it took me decades to expunge a certain coy femininity

I write, Listen, it's not what you're thinking

Listen, it's *exactly* what you're thinking

I write, Mind your own beeswax. Then I google "beeswax," learn that in the 1800s women used beeswax to cover up their smallpox scars, a kind of proto-foundation, thus if some busybody got all up in your face, you told them, "Mind your own beeswax"

B.A., you're stalling

I write, In all this time I've never brought myself to post a photo of us, heads tilting cheek-to-cheek, arms hugging each other's warm, bare shoulders, sharing our likeness for all to see, not even on her birthday can I bring myself to do it, although when others post Heavenly Birthdays, I always like them

I write, The autopsy lists the immediate cause of death as pneumonia, but who dies of pneumonia, really, in their thirties, in the America of the Twenty-First Century—to be more specific, in the metropolis of Chicago in the Year of Our Lord Two-Thousand-and-Eight

Significant contributing conditions include chronic tobacco use, fatty liver, elevated blood alcohol concentration, undernourishment

I write, I've always felt her death was at least 13% a suicide, but maybe she didn't choose death even a little bit, maybe she was just so used to getting away with everything, maybe she couldn't believe she'd ever have to pay, flashing her devil-may-care grin over her shoulder as she fishtailed on her Big Wheel, leaving me behind in a spray of gravel, me always running, running to catch up

I write, My sweet brother-in-law—at that point, they'd been married only a year—called me first, that cold October morning, when he woke and discovered that she hadn't

That was the first time I heard her referred to as *her body*, as in *When I touched her body, it was already cold*

Tommy came running when I started screaming

Later, we'd discover that the last thing my sister did on her last night on earth was google "flu symptoms." You see, she was unemployed, so she was uninsured, so she self-diagnosed

I write, I've always felt my sister's death was at least 13% a homicide, a homicide perpetrated by the American health care system

I write, We didn't have a grave for her, no pre-purchased site. A family friend took pity, offered us a spare plot in the Catholic cemetery. Bonus: the plot was double depth, meaning my sister was buried on the bottom and my mother can one day lie down on top. A day approaching soon. The stone above my sister's grave has room to bear my mother's name. My sister forever trapped under our mother's Catholic thumb. Mother with the last laugh, if Alzheimer's hadn't robbed her even of laughter

I write, My sister, back in high school, was so skilled at sneaking out. For instance, the alarm-clock caper. Her curfew was eleven, mother set her alarm clock for eleven and placed it on the stairs, then went to bed, forcing my sister to be home by curfew to turn it off, or it'd wake our mom. That's where I came in, clutching the five dollars she'd given me as bribe, holding my breath down the creaky steps to switch the alarm to off. Worked like clockwork, it did, until the dawn mom woke and went to fetch the

newspaper from the driveway. And found it pinned beneath my sister's tire, her car's flank still warm
We both got grounded, big time, for that little stunt
I write, No sneaking out now, big sis. And while you skipped out on our mother's entire illness, guess what, your turn is coming. Our mother lying down on top of you and maddeningly repeating the same question over and over, not just for hours, but for eternity: your fate worse than death
You, wedged firmly as a newspaper beneath a car tire
You, grounded
I write, The four stages of pneumonia are congestion, red hepatization, gray hepatization, and resolution. Resolution is when symptoms improve and the sufferer returns to health. But we have no resolution in Cook County Case 08-OCT-0195
I write, Undernourishment, I can't even. It was always so important to be slim. I suppose she decided to reserve her calories for Miller Lite and Three Buck Chuck
Even now I'm screaming and Tommy is running
Even now I only 98.3% believe she's dead
I write, How dare you people expect me to explain my sister's death to you, a thing I've never successfully explained even *once* to myself
I write, Even now, if it would help, even now I would gladly press my lips to your corpsey lips, my sister, expand your clotted lungs with my strong lungs, with my pure air, I would give you the kiss of life, I would give you everything I've saved inside, everything I've hoarded

Breathe

The Roomies

1.
A rare and beautiful purple hollyhock, Baker's globe mallow, emerges in the forests of Oregon and California, but only after a forest fire. Its seed requires intense heat to germinate. Interestingly, this hollyhock has been found in forests where a fire hadn't previously occurred for one hundred years, proving the seeds can remain dormant for a century before being triggered by a blaze.

A rare and ugly vein, the Devil Vein, emerges on my forehead, but only during Wild Women's Weekends. That's when I'm with my roomies. And when I'm with my roomies, I laugh. I laugh so hard that a usually dormant vein pops into prominence above the bridge of my nose, branching off right and left before resuming its upward path toward my hairline, forming a pitchfork.

See what I'm getting at? The roomies are my forest fire. They bring out the devil in me.

2.
Four of the five of us met during college orientation—this was at the University of Notre Dame, August 1989. Actually, freshman year, only two of us were roomies: Beth and Carmen. I lived next door. Denise lived one flight up, Laura close by. I suppose, had we been placed in other dorms, we would have formed other friendships, perhaps equally strong. But looking back, it's hard not to see our fellowship as fated as Frodo's.

Every fifth year we meet at Notre Dame for our class reunion. In between, we create our own. Our early post-ND years were rich with weddings: Laura's and later Beth's in Massachusetts; Carmen's in South Bend; mine in Chicago; and Denise's in a castle in Ireland.

Or the weddings of our close guy friends: Danny's in Indianapolis, Lloyd's at the Jersey Shore. In subsequent years, we converged on each other's homes. (Oh my pride when the roomies came here to Mississippi and closed City Grocery. The mythical and beautiful roomies. I felt like I'd unleashed a quartet of Fireball-shooting unicorns.) Sometimes we choose an ND football game. Mostly we just pick a city on the East Coast. Beth, Denise, and Laura drive there, and Carm and I fly, and we split our two plane tickets five ways. We've done Boston three times and NYC twice in this manner, as well as Frye Island and Portland, Maine; Newport, Rhode Island; the Jersey Shore; and Martha's Vineyard.

3.

Our fifteenth reunion. It's late, after the class banquet, and we're driving back to our hotel. We've just learned that Club 23, one of our two favorite bars, is scheduled for demolition. The club was a true dive, a dark-paneled seventies ranch with carpet—carpet, in a bar—but we loved the owner, Mo Hussein, and collected great memories there.

Once, carrying two full pitchers down the stairs into the basement rec room, I lost my footing and skidded to the bottom on my bum. The tables of drinkers looked down where I sprawled, still holding the pitchers. I braced for heckling. Instead I received an ovation. I'd fallen down the stairs, sure, but I hadn't spilled the beer. "The Stairmaster": my nickname for a few weeks.

Years later, cowriting with my husband a novel set during Prohibition, I'd name our speakeasy Club 23 and christen the bartender Mo.

But now the club is to be demolished. Demoed. De-Mo-ed.

"Let's drive by," suggests Beth. "For old times' sake."

So we do, mournfully rolling past, noting the CLOSED sign. But from the side window, a light glows.

Without pausing to consult, Denise whips the car behind the club. "We've *got* to check this out," she orders.

At the stoop, we hear music, so Denise pounds on the door. Immediately the music stops. For a long, tense moment nothing happens. Finally, the lock clanks, the chain rattles. The door cracks open an inch and two dark eyes peek out.

It's been fifteen years, but people tend to remember the roomies. Especially the loud ones. "Hey," calls Mo brightly. "It's Beth and Denise!"

Next thing you know, we five are hustled inside, and the door is bolted again. Before us, a handful of locals gather around a guitarist. We've just magically stumbled upon Mo's secret goodbye party for his beloved bar. He mixes us some free cocktails and we join the group singing with the guitarist, who starts in with Pearl Jam's "Elderly Woman Behind the Counter in a Small Town." It's one of those times when art harmonizes with reality. The song is about the bittersweet passing of time, about being recognized again after many years, about the things that fade and the things that don't. We are belting out the words, swaying with these strangers / new best friends.

We croon Bon Jovi, and Aerosmith, and Radiohead, and Led Zepplin (the guitarist's oeuvre limited, I'm afraid, to nineties testosterone rock, but we know all the lyrics, don't we, despite ourselves).

Later, much later, when we leave, we stand for a moment in the deserted parking lot, quiet, companionable, a touch melancholy. Laura notices that you can see the Golden Dome, the beloved landmark of the university, between the buildings. She says, "Look, there's some kind of new spotlight."

And indeed there is—a pink light glows on the east side of the dome.

"Oh my God," says Denise, breaking our reverie. "That's not a spotlight. That's *the sunrise.*"

I go to bed at 10 p.m. these days; I didn't even know I *could* stay up all night. But somehow, with the roomies, anything's possible, including, before the wrecking ball swings through the hallowed halls and carpeted floors of Club 23, singing ourselves into sunrise.

4.

I'm a writer now, and I teach writing. My husband's a writer. Most of our friends are writers. I didn't mean for my world to shrink like this, but my colleagues are great, and Tommy and I go to a lot of conferences with other writers, so over the years, our social circle has grown less occupationally diverse.

Which is one more reason to value the roomies. They enlarge me.

Can I brag on them? You saw us meeting in the halls of ND in '89. Let me present them as grown women.

Laura teaches biology at a prep school in Massachusetts. She and her husband live on the campus with their three kids, flip houses in their spare time. At ND she wanted to become a vet before discovering her vocation, making science come alive for teens. She still loves animals, especially aquatic ones. She's a scuba instructor and every spring break takes her students diving at exotic locales to inspire them to love—and protect—the ocean's creatures.

Beth is the director of social work for the largest prison in Massachusetts, an hour from where she lives with her husband and three hockey-warrior daughters. She's five foot one, a redhead, and fierce (once, on spring break, we were in a beach bar that held a beer-chugging contest; Beth defeated three giant bartenders in the semifinals). It's that same spark plug who now keeps those medium-security inmates in line. A favorite story: At her facility, an inmate seeks counseling by filling out a card with a box to request his area of need, say, anger management or addiction recovery. One such card became the delight of Beth's colleagues. For his area of need, he wrote, "Just not the redhead. Please, God, anyone but the redhead."

Denise, former captain of the ND soccer team, is the CMO of a huge financial outfit, a Fortune 500 company. Her life seems both incredibly foreign and incredibly glamorous. I might email her from my small town in Mississippi, where I'm working to unwedge a gummy bear from the bell of my daughter's trumpet. She might email back from Argentina, where she's checking on the production of one of her commercials, or Scotland, where she's golfing with her husband, or a college in the US where she's giving a motivational speech to student athletes. She lives weekdays in the West Village, weekends on the coast of Maine.

Carmen, stay-at-home mother of five, has perhaps the hardest job: stay-at-home mother of five. She also has another job that doesn't have a title, but should. She's married to the vice president of University Relations, which means she's deeply involved in campus life. She's the hostess of countless events, but a hostess motivated by compassion, not social climbing. Carmen is Brazilian, and her favorite folks to host are the international students, having been one herself. Once she told me a WWW had snuck up on her because just a few days earlier she and her husband moved their son into his ND dorm to start his first year. "Also, we hosted a brunch during orientation for some incoming international students," she added. "How many?" I asked, thinking it would be challenging to host ten or twelve strangers while moving a son into his dorm and preparing for our trip. "Oh, two hundred and fifty," she answered.

She didn't seem to think that was anything remarkable. That's Carm for you. Remarkable.

Thus, I continue my remarks.

5.

While at ND, I was the only roomie whose family was within driving distance. That's why, for short breaks like Easter, the roomies would decamp to my house, in Lake Forest, IL. My parents had always planned elaborate Easter egg hunts for my sister and me, and now they quintupled their efforts.

So while the primary branch of our ND family tree is between roommates, soon "roomies to parents" and "roomies to sister" rooted.

The tree branched out from there. Jump ahead to 2009, when I'm awarded a Fulbright to Brazil to study the poetry of Elizabeth Bishop. My husband and children and I visited Carmen's parents in São Paulo. So another limb of the tree grew, roomie to parent without the child-roomie present.

And when Carmen's singer-songwriter daughter, Bela, performed at a music festival in Illinois, my mom drove the thirty minutes to hear her. Now we have the parent-of-roomie to child-of-roomie connection.

This enmeshing is why, when we get together, we can pick up in medias res. It's not just that we know each roomie's husband; we know the string of boyfriends before the husband. It's not just that we know each other's parents, siblings, children; we know each other's parents' siblings, and siblings' children.

It's not just that I'm known by these women. It's that I'm known deeply, comprehensively, compassionately. It's incredibly grounding to be known—and, despite being known, to be loved.

Already my arms are greedy to hold the grandbabies of my roomies.

6.

Though it's fair to add that our friendship puts a lot of pressure on itself. When I look back at WWWs, I recall various tensions. Lots of tears—often from me, I'm a crier—our weekends so long anticipated, so fraught and emotional. It's natural that a twenty-eight-year friendship among five women would have its arguments, rivalries, resentments. We've hurt and disappointed each other. We've taken the great gift that is our friendship for granted. But mostly what I think of is how much we've been through.

One of us got in a near-fatal car accident, so nearly fatal she entered a coma and received last rites. One of us almost died in childbirth. One of us had a fetus that had to be operated on in utero, a miracle operation so new and risky at the time that it was documented in medical journals. One of us left Catholicism. One of us lost an estranged parent to alcoholism. One of us lost a beloved parent to cancer. One of us had a sibling with addiction issues. One of us had a sibling get divorced. One of us had a sibling die. One of us had a child who suffered from a mental health condition. One of us drank too much and had to get sober.

During these times, we were with each other, knowing and known.

7.

New York City, Denise's fortieth birthday, at the super-trendy gastropub, the Spotted Pig. The roomies arrived, checked into the hotel, started getting ready, preparations a bit more complicated for Carmen and me, both of us with babies at home. Happy memories of the party? Yes. But surprisingly, the happiest: sitting next to Carm on the hotel bed, laughing and catching up after twelve months apart, both of us bare-chested and strapped to wheezing suctioning tubes, pumping breast milk so we could go boogie at Denise's fortieth.

8.

When I'm on book tour, if they're within driving distance, they come. And oh, an auditorium with the roomies is an entirely sunnier place.

I look up from the page I'm reading, and sometimes I see, blossoming through, the teenage girls who'd sit cross-legged on the dorm room floor, listening to the poem I was about to nervously hand in for poetry workshop.

If I tell you they are as beautiful to me now as they were then, you will say sentimentality clouds my vision. But it's worse than that, actually. I find them *more* beautiful. Intimacy is beautiful, and what's more intimate than being privy to a body's ripenings? The crow's-feet. The laugh lines. Age spots. Reading glasses. Scars: cesarean, hysterectomy. The one whose right hip aches because for years she carried a child there. The one whose back aches because she was almost killed in a car accident. Proof of life. Proof of our lucky lives.

9.

One of us lost a sibling. I said that already.

What I didn't say: it was me. My sibling. My only. My Julie. She died without warning, nine years ago this month. Something shorted out in my brain when she died. I mean, on some neurological level, my thinking broke. Those days are mostly lost to me, though sometimes an image ruptures through so violently I live again in the dark hours of her death.

But what I really want to tell you is this: They came. The roomies came. They were with me at the funeral and they were with me after. I reached for them the way a drowning woman reaches for a life raft.

One way they kept me from going under was by bringing me laughter, which might sound strange, but everything was strange, I was a strange stranger. At one point we were at my mom's house and the roomies started ripping on Carmen's handbag. Probably Carm packed in a rush and God knows she had other things (me) on her mind, but she'd paired her tasteful black funeral dress with a tasteless, oversized, out-of-season purse decorated with overlapping leather disks in pink, aqua, and yellow. I think we roasted that handbag for a solid ten minutes. I remember Denise at one point threading her arm through it and mock-strutting the catwalk: "Nothing says *I'm grieving* like a dead armadillo dangling from your shoulder." Laughter, laughter, my pitchfork throbbing, tears streaming from my helpless, hopeless eyes.

10.

Tommy grew up in the woods of blue-collar Alabama, in a family of hunters and mechanics. The first in his family to earn a college degree, he worked days at a chemical waste factory, a sandblasting grit factory, and a hospital morgue, all so he could take night school literature classes. Earning his BA cost him seven years and a healthy back. I'm prouder of his degree from that small local college than I am of my ND diploma.

Tommy found it hard to believe my roomies would feel the same way, however, and was intimidated when we gathered. "They're not snobs," I assured him. "They love you." He just sighed and shook his head.

Tommy grew up a baseball fan, but because his family didn't travel, he'd hardly been to a game. After Wrigley Field, where we had our rehearsal dinner, his greatest wish was to see Fenway. It was Laura, I think, who came up with the idea to surprise him with Red Sox tickets. So we all met up in Boston with our husbands. When we clambered aboard the T, the only thing Tommy knew was that we were heading to an Irish pub. He glanced at the train map. "Wow," he whispered, "this T goes to Fenway!" He was excited to even pass by the long-dreamed-of stadium.

"Yes," I told him, "the pub's right near there."

"Huh," he said. "How cool that we'll be nearby."

Some revelers boarded the T in Red Sox jerseys, clearly Fenway-bound. At the next stop, a few more fans squeezed on, waving foam fingers. Tommy gazed at them wistfully and sighed.

"What is it, hon?" I asked.

"It's just—to be so close, you know? So close, and on game night. I'm kind of . . . aching a little."

I nodded and squeezed his arm, struggling to swallow the secret.

When we reached Fenway, Tommy glanced longingly over his shoulder at the stadium as I herded him into the pub. Where my roomies presented him with tickets.

Unbelieving, at first, and then so boyishly, unabashedly joyful: "We're going to the game?" He looked around at the conspiring smiles. "You—you planned this—for me?"

Well, I already told you I'm a crier. You can picture what I was doing right about then.

Of course, this is a roomie story, so there's an addendum that nudges it from pathos to comedy. An old-school Irishman was tending bar and later asked Tommy about the ruckus. Tommy explained, and though the bartender had to be weary of tourists, he laid a hand on Tommy's shoulder, clearly moved. "That's brilliant," he said in his brogue. He set out two enormous shot glasses. "Me and you, we're gonna drink a whiskey." He took a bottle from the highest shelf and filled the glasses to the brim. "To friendship," he said, then hoisted his glass.

Tommy doesn't drink whiskey. And he certainly can't shoot a tumbler of it. But, flush with exhilaration—the roomies like him! The bartender likes him!—he toasted glasses and threw the whiskey back. One-Mississippi, two-Mississippi. Then, the whiskey rebellion. He leaned over the bar and puked the whiskey back into the giant shot glass, filling it neatly to the brim.

"Aye, mate," the bartender said sadly, removing the glass to the sink. "Ye needn't go recycling a fine whiskey."

11.

How many miles, I wonder, have Denise and I clocked, running side by side? While students, we'd run the two campus lakes in a figure eight, sometimes for exercise, sometimes to relieve stress after her lost soccer game or my poorly received poem. In 1998, we ran the Chicago Marathon together (well, technically, I ran it about an hour behind her, but still). Every WWW, too, we run, and if we can get to ND, we run, and we are the same two humans on the same two sets of legs figure-eighting the same two lakes, a fact that feels equally banal and profound. Each time, I surge with gratitude that the peculiar joy of hurtling a body through space is still accessible to us, may it always be so.

But it *won't* always be so. There will come a time—if we are lucky enough to live long enough—when we'll have to give up running the lakes. And a time after that when we'll give up walking them. We'll join those on the benches at the lake's edge, watching the runners whiz by. But the vision I indulge in provides solace: the five of us, cotton-haired, waiting for the clouds to clear so the sunset can sorbet-smear the water. Maybe we need two benches for our widened backsides. Maybe there are a few canes resting between our arthritic knees. We're watching the geese, a few turtles lined up on a branch, and beyond that, the reflection of the Golden Dome. We're talking, of course, catching each other up on our grandchildren's shenanigans. Denise cracks a joke and we bark a laugh that startles a goose into flight, which causes the turtles to plop into the water in rapid succession, like a string of firecrackers. The sun pries open the clouds, runs its fingers over our laughing faces, accentuating—on one lined brow—the sign of the devil, a pitchfork coming into relief.

Your Mother Falls Again and Breaks Her Other Hip

Remember how you used to hate it when someone pulled an Irish goodbye?

Inheritance

It won't be long before I have my mother's rings.

I already have her fingers.

Married Love: Because I've Been French Kissing Him for Twenty-Nine Years

I discern that earlier, during dinner, my husband must have bitten his tongue.

I discern this after dinner, with my tongue.

What I Think About When Someone Says They're Estranged from Their Sibling

Maybe, if you were still alive, we also wouldn't be close. Maybe we wouldn't even like each other. Maybe I'd see your name on my phone and groan, roll my eyes at my husband, who would murmur sympathetically, *You have to talk to her sometime.* Maybe we'd live on different coasts. Maybe *that* wouldn't feel far enough. Maybe we'd dread Thanksgiving, drink our way through it, promising ourselves, *Three hundred and sixty-four days before I have to see her again.* Maybe, hungover the next morning on the toilet dribbling saffron-colored pee, I'd think stupidly of the joke about how you can pick your nose but you can't pick your family. Maybe your death is what perfected you, the cause célèbre on which I can pin any problems, your death my excuse, your death unquestionably the source of my *weltschmerz*, my longing, my loneliness, my lack, my cherished belief that I've been robbed. Robbed of my boon companion. Maybe your death is my boon. Maybe it's freed me to craft the perfect voodoo doll, a doll I pose with her arms out, reaching for my embrace. Maybe every poem I write about missing you becomes, after I pin it through your doll heart, another pretty petticoat, another layer of myth. You died before we strangered ourselves. Before I got a chance to thank you.

Most Days Are Days like This

If you have gin, there's no tonic, if you have tonic, there's no gin, and if you by chance have both, for sure you lack a lime. No lime, not even rattling at the back of the crisper, juiceless as a stone, dark and bitter as a testicle of Jehovah. Most days, except the day of your first big writers' conference. At the base of the mountain you passed the sign LAST LIQUOR FOR 30 MILES, so you pulled off. Hours later, after the reception, someone organized an afterparty, but by the time you got there—writers milling about, admiring the stars, congenially flirting—the booze was gone. You, meanwhile, were starstruck, working hard at looking chill, when up walks Tim O'Brien, that's right, Tim fucking O'Brien, a man who'd written a book so beautiful it gave you paper cuts, a book from which you knew whole passages by heart, though you said none of this to him, in fact you were bereft of words entirely. That's when he murmured to no one in particular, "I could really go for a gin and tonic." You popped your trunk. You handed him the gin, then the tonic, he gawked like you were the merciful angel of juniper, which you were, your wings surely glowing in the limelight emitting from your trunk when, for your final trick, you held aloft the lime. "Even the lime!" he crowed, boyish in his baseball cap. You understood, in that moment, all your sins had been redeemed. Most days are days in which you dryly tote up all your petty failures, but let's not dismiss the time you produced a lime for Tim O'Brien.

Making Plans with Friends

In college, Lloyd was perfect boyfriend material—sweet, smart, funny, and handsome. But you never dated: no chemistry. Instead, you became friends. In those days, you were always buffeted about by love, alternating unsuitable boyfriends with unrequited crushes. Meanwhile, you watched your roommates happily pairing off. Your despair arose not so much from the prospect of being single forever as from the prospect of never having children. Even then, you stared at babies in the grocery store.

Lloyd, meanwhile, was enduring his own bad luck in love. You'd commiserate, exchange war stories. Lloyd also wanted a family and was beginning to doubt its likelihood. Which was crazy: anyone could see he'd make a great husband and father. At some point, one of you—and now it's thirty-five years later, so neither of you can remember who—came up with The Plan. You'd continue putting yourselves out there, sure. But if you were losers and loveless at thirty—an age that seemed impossibly geriatric—you'd meet up and mess around until you had kids. You kept this plan from your roommates, but sometimes when you and Lloyd were alone, one of you would allude to it and the other would grin. Of course, in time, you both found great spouses and had three kids apiece. But for years the two of you—goal-oriented and type A—took comfort from The Plan.

And now you've got an Updated Plan. Again, kept from your roomies. For the past several years, you and Lloyd have watched Alzheimer's avalanche your mothers, have watched it bury them alive. When acquaintances ask how your mom is doing, you always say she's fine, because the truth is too ugly. You reserve the ugly truth for Lloyd. You commiserate, exchange war stories. When he phoned last month to say his mom had finally died, he had the grace not to be shocked when these words tumbled from your mouth: "I'm jealous." All he said was, "I know, honey. I know."

So he remains your perfect collaborator. A hundred times, when talking about the drawn-out misery of these deaths, you've vowed to each other: *Not me. Not like that.* You've given serious consideration to alternatives, and both have communicated your wishes. Lloyd: gun. You: pills.

But what if, when the time comes, his finger is too weak to pull the trigger? What if you can't count the pills or remember to swallow them?

Relax: he understands the value of a plan, your former-future-baby-daddy, turned current-future-murderer. He'll have figured out your dosage. You'll know how to shoot the gun.

Married Love: Addendum to "Making Plans with Friends"

You know it would never actually come to that, says your husband.

Why not? you ask. You don't think Lloyd would murder me?

It's not that. It's that—well, if you needed murdering, I'd be the one to murder you.

Oh, sweetheart, you say. You could never murder me. You love me too much to murder me.

No, your husband says. I love you so much that I *would* murder you. It would have to be me, with you, at the very end, murdering you.

That's the most romantic thing, you say, and mean it.

And then you both laugh for a long time.

Dear Viewer of My Naked Body

My husband and I were heading to a dinner party hosted by our old friends John T. and Blair. As Tommy drove, I googled "Robert Townsend painter"—our new friends, Dave and Alison, had said they were bringing their artist friend from Arizona, and I wanted to check out his work.

The top hit was an oil painting with a fun, mid-century vibe, saturated with bright color, featuring a dark-haired woman with a high bouffant, cat's-eye glasses, and a polyester sixties minidress. I was instantly smitten by her, but not because she was some ravishing beauty—she was middle-age-ish, shortish, stoutish. But she radiated joy. Her knockout, crooked smile was aimed squarely at the camera, or whoever was holding it. Now I was the beneficiary of that loving look. Basically, it was a stupidly good painting, and the longer I looked at it, the happier I felt. "Damn," I said, and showed Tommy at a stoplight. "Damn," he agreed.

Rob himself, when I met him at the party, lacked his subject's high-wattage dazzle—I think he was wearing jeans and a plain button-down—and initially was a bit subdued. Though it's hard to remain subdued at John T. and Blair's parties, lots of laughter and silliness, incredible food, a bunch of natural storytellers one-upping each other, a vintage coupe glass you never see the bottom of. They are artists, John T. and Blair; the former with words, the second with paint. But they are also artists of the evening. Connoisseurs of the Cocktail Hour. Guardians of the Gathering.

Rob wasn't one to elbow his way into the storytelling World Cup, but all night I'd been wondering about the woman from the painting, and when a silence opened, I asked about her.

"Ah," he said, and smiled. "That's Helen."

We settled back for a good story and got one. A decade prior, he told us, he'd made an impulse bid on eBay for a collection of vintage Kodachrome slides. When they arrived, he discovered all three thousand slides were of the same woman, decades of her adulthood in one box, her celebrations and vacations and domestic relaxations. Often she was with the same man, sometimes in coordinating plaid pantsuits, and Rob rightly guessed him to be her husband. But whether leaning against a vintage Chrysler with her hubby or toasting martini glasses with her gal pals, that same life-loving woman commanded his gaze, her pleasure in her existence radically unquestioned.

Rob began painting her, which made him more determined to learn her identity. He knew the slides had come from an estate sale in Indiana. His clue arrived via a slide in which she was wearing a name tag: Helen. Sleuth work led him to her nieces, who were only too glad to see their beloved aunt, recently deceased, captured in her Technicolor glory.

For the next eight years, Rob painted Helen exclusively. His large, highly detailed, labor-intensive oils re-created Helen's vacation photos, down to the small, pebbled scree of the desert slope behind her strappy sandals, a scree that took him thirteen days to paint. He also re-created her vacations, traveling to the places where she'd been. His quest eventually became the subject of a documentary, *My Indiana Muse*.

Amazing, we said, and asked about seeing the documentary, which Rob promised to send.

Someone asked him how long he'd continue to paint Helen.

Actually, Rob said, he'd recently sensed that the Helen series was perhaps coming to an end. That's one reason he was traveling.

How long was he staying in Mississippi? we wanted to know.

Something about that lively evening had made something in him decide something about us. "I'm here for a short visit now," he said, "but I'm coming back next week, and sticking around for a bit." Maybe testing it out, I'm not sure.

Did he know what he'd paint next?

At first, he answered vaguely. But a bit later, he offered, "I'm starting a series of nudes. I'm looking for models to photograph when I return to town. If you know of anyone . . ."

At the evening's end, he handed out business cards. I took one. By that point, I hadn't seen the bottom of my vintage coupe in a very long time.

The next morning, when the sober light of Sunday pierced my blinds, I picked up my discarded dress from the floor, shook it out, and found, in a lumpy pocket, Rob's creased business card.

I tossed it in the garbage as we headed out to church.

That Rob's artistic trajectory would evolve to the painting of nudes would surprise anyone familiar with his early work, which, according to the Sullivan Goss Gallery, features "highly finished images of the icons of an American Pop mythology." Often closely cropped, the objects he elevates from bygone eras—bottle caps, lollipops, matchbooks—evoke nostalgia. They are celebrated quite separately from their human usefulness—there is no elbow propped in the window of the Dodge Dart, no fingers rifling the vintage travel brochures, no fork puncturing the sunny wedge of lemon meringue. They are not besmirched by flesh or function.

Rob would have had buyers for these astonishing feats of photorealism until he hung up his palette. But one fateful day, his path took a sharp right, courtesy of that box of vintage slides. Again,

Rob could have stuck with his new subject for the rest of the career. Who doesn't need a little Helen in their life?

But after several years, he observed two things.

First, when painting Helen, he was "playing one note on the piano, a joyful, lighthearted note, a note I loved playing." Nevertheless, it was only one note. Rob's a philosophical person. You don't have to converse with him long before you find yourself sifting below the small talk. Maybe that's why he was so drawn to Helen, now that I think of it; her effervescence balances his gravitas.

He began considering what other notes he wanted to play.

At the same time, he noticed that, while he still enjoyed painting Helen, the locus of his enjoyment had shifted. Initially, because he'd come to Helen from his Pop Art background, he loved to paint her kitten heels and Hawaiian prints. But several years in, Rob found himself happier painting her hand than her handbag. Happier painting her neck than her necklace. Happiest of all painting her face: "When we see faces," he'd tell me later, "we're hardwired to feel a deeper connection." If he got rid of everything decorative, he wondered, would this connection deepen even further? The body, he realized, was his destination. The body would allow him to investigate the question that drives him: What makes us human?

Rob says that when he arrived in Oxford, he hadn't planned on painting Oxford nudes. He was simply cogitating on painting nudes. Maybe in France, where he had a connection to a naturalist community. It probably wouldn't be hard to talk people into being photographed in the buff when they already gardened, shopped, rode bicycles, and ate escargots in the buff.

But something unexpected happened when Rob arrived in

Oxford. He puts it simply: "I fell in love." Though doing so made his task a good bit more challenging. He had to—literally—charm the pants off us.

Twelve of us, eventually, in the same small town of Oxford, Mississippi—population 27,531. Not every one of these twelve subjects knows every other subject, but we all know some. If you lived here, you would know some, too. One might hand you an old-fashioned over his marble-topped bar. Another might Velcro the blood-pressure sleeve to your bicep and pump it snug. One might lower a plate of shrimp and grits to your white-linen draped table. One might teach you how to do "the hundreds" in Pilates. One might be your child's English professor. That last one might be me.

WHY I (EVENTUALLY) POSED

1. I like art. I think there should be more of it.
2. I like Rob. I like Rob, and I like his work, and I like his vision for his work. I like how he'd spoken of painting Helen as an honor. In *My Indiana Muse*, we see Helen through Rob's eyes, and we all develop crushes on her. But he's the one who first apprehended her star power, he's the one who recognized her lovability. That's a tremendous act of perception.
3. Rob expressed a wish for imperfect bodies. He said normally the people eager to pose are twenty and physically perfect. But perfection, Rob said, is boring.
4. Well now, I happen to *have* an imperfect body. It's right here, under my dress. And if I rail against an ethos that obsesses over youth—if I detest the cultural pressure to lift, tuck, plump, inject, and laser—if I reject the mandate to needle botulism

between my brows to erase my "thinkle"—if I believe that one way we could reduce this pressure to conform to an impossible ideal would be to see bodies of all shapes, sizes, colors, and levels of ability represented without shame, should I not then offer the one imperfect body that's mine to offer? If I hate that middle-aged women are looked *through*, should I not then offer one to be looked *at*? (I dare you to look through my portrait, by the way. First, I'm seven feet tall. Second, I'm framed in fluorescent pink.)

5. The year prior, turning fifty in the darkest depth of Covid, I pledged that if the pandemic ever ended, I would say *yes* to things that scare me. Reach deep into the Fuck It Bucket. "NO REGERTS," as my middle child, at the age of eight, Sharpied on his forearm, to show me the tattoo he planned on having inked as soon as he was legal.

"The nude," Rob would tell me later on the phone, "is the most honest version of the most important subject."

Honesty centers his approach. His nudes aren't sensualized, aren't glamorized. Rob's women are not posed like Raphael's *The Three Graces*, beauties with weight shifted onto one leg so the other can draw in softly, emphasizing curvy hips, sinuous lines. No, we're not posed like the Three Graces as painted by Raphael, nor like the Three Graces as painted by Rubens, nor Brueghel the Elder, nor Brueghel the Younger—the Three Graces being so often painted by male artists throughout history that comedian Hannah Gadsby concludes, "Dancing naked in groups of three in the forest is the number one hobby of women of all time."

No, not the Three Graces. We are graceless, and alone.

Or all who'd posed before me were alone, except for Alison. I heard she'd posed with her BFF, both of them laughing. I figured maybe that was her prerogative for hosting these shoots at her house, as well as having to angle the dang light reflector on the rest of us nekkid folks. But now that I've seen their double portrait, I think that her beautiful friend, whom I don't know, must have appreciated having a hand to squeeze as she bared her double mastectomy.

Unlike Alison and her friend, I was squared toward the camera, arms at my sides, hair behind my back so I couldn't even drape it to hide my naughty bits. No YouTuber's "How to Look Sexy in Photos!!" could save me now. No angle-your-foot-to-lengthen-your-leg. No visual Spanx. Most nudes are arranged in poses that feel avoidant, Rob explained, and in diffused light, which rids skin of cellulite and wrinkles. Rob desired "warts and all," and achieved his desire with my sun-freckled Irish skin: proof of life.

Larger than life, actually. The portraits are larger than life. Rob wanted, he said, a mirroring effect: whoever confronts the portrait is confronted. Viewers are compelled to see themselves in the other.

Here's something I'm wondering. Would Rob's portraits read differently if we were twelve New Yorkers, say, instead of twelve recognizable residents from the same small town in a conservative state? If we were accustomed to being naked, if we were nudists from that French village? If we were professional artist's models, if we answered an ad on Craigslist, in order to get paid?

Does our startling vulnerability show, does it make any blooming difference?

ꕥ

We did get paid, though I didn't know that in advance, and if I *had* known, it would only have made me less likely to pose.

We'd agreed on a time for the photo shoot at Dave and Alison's, midday, between my classes at the university. When I pulled into their driveway, I could see a giant lightbox had been erected on the lawn, a wooden frame wrapped in panels of white fabric, the top open to the sun, which allowed Rob to use natural light but also provided privacy for the models. A sign in the grass diverted UPS drivers to a side door, which I figured ensured that the models wouldn't be alarmed by some brown shirt requiring a signature.

Inside the house, we chatted—me nervously—and then Alison led me to the elegant bathroom where a white terry cloth robe was folded, newly purchased, its sash belted. I stripped quickly, avoiding the mirror's seductive invitation to chicken out. I cinched the robe and they led me outside to the enclosure. The only furniture was a standing coatrack on which to hang my robe, a rack much too thin to hide behind. Rob lifted his camera.

Whenever you're ready.

I undid the sash, slipped out of the robe, hung it on the hook, and turned around.

My grammar school teacher Ms. Naylon detested inaccuracies of language. Absolute states of matter, she asserted, are absolute. Water couldn't be "very boiling," ice couldn't be "very freezing," a woman couldn't be "very pregnant." I'm sorry, Ms. Naylon, but standing there under the brightest possible midday Mississippi sun, I was not naked, I was very, *very* naked. There was nothing to do with my hands. Rob's shutter clicked, with him occasionally advising Alison to angle the light reflector to bounce the sun on me, though the sun itself was doing a good job, making me squint, which I ruefully understood would only deepen my laugh lines.

Then it was over. In less than ten minutes. I re-belted my robe and was led back inside and reentered the bathroom and re-donned my dress. When I came out, I was offered coffee and we chatted about weekend plans (me, nervously). Rob took out a copy of my latest book and said some kind things and asked me to inscribe it. As I did, I thought—How *nice*. How nice of him to read my book. He didn't have to, but his doing so makes our exchange less transactional, more artist-to-artist.

That's when he said there was a check on the counter for three hundred dollars.

I make bad jokes when I'm nervous. "Why don't you just leave it on my nightstand like the other men I strip for?"

Rob has a large, open face, a large, open brow, and a hurt look flickered across it.

All the work he'd done to ensure that models felt safe and respected: he'd arranged the photo shoots not to overlap to protect our privacy and built the sheeted enclosure and diverted the UPS driver and purchased new bathrobes and kept Alison with us at all times, he'd done all of that and he'd read my book to boot, and I had to go and crack a stupid joke. I had to go and sully it.

But I still drove away abuzz in euphoria or adrenaline or something. I had done it, this thing I wasn't sure I could do. Returning to campus to teach, I took a wrong turn, though I knew the way. That's how keyed up I was. I parked in the same spot I'd left not an hour earlier, surprised it was still there, as though the world hadn't shifted.

"You can't force people to have compassion," Rob would tell me later, when I'd already been painted and the series was well underway. "But we should be able to see ourselves in any other person, in any gender or age or body." He paused, selecting his words with care. "I think for me, painting nudes is an exercise in increasing empathy."

Maybe that explains my reaction upon first viewing my portrait, which pinged into my inbox as an attachment, Rob's subject heading, "Finished painting," causing me to die a little. Though I didn't regret posing exactly, I dreaded anyone seeing my portrait. I dreaded their judgment, judgment of both my body and my decision to bare it. (Here I note the sad freedom of already having lost my father and sister, and pretty much having lost my mother to Alzheimer's—I no longer need to seek their approval. For all three would have denied it.)

Waiting for the image to load, I proceeded with my dying.

I had anticipated that seeing my portrait would incite a harsh confrontation of my flaws.

What surprised me is that, while critique did occur, it wasn't my primary reaction.

My primary reaction was awe.

What sorcery is this, what magic trick, to flatten a three-dimensional woman onto a canvas and, with only pigments and linseed oil, make her look *exactly* like herself?

Like, *exactly.*

Like, *exactly* exactly.

I'm trying to re-create my sonic boom upon seeing the portrait. Simply put: I think first I recognized myself, and then I recognized my humanity.

Look at my bunions, I remember thinking with a giddy delight.

My feet are ugly with an ugliness I've earned honestly, from years of running, and less honestly, from years of wearing high heels.

When we use poses, filters, and diffused light to distract, correct, or erase, we're complicit in the lie of perfection, while also cognizant of failing to meet the very criteria we're reinforcing.

Rob, through his refusal to distract, correct, or erase my imperfections, dignified them. Through his attention, he dignified them.

I think I experienced the empathy he spoke of. Empathy for the human. Empathy for the bunion.

Does it appear I'm making too much of posing nude? Younger generations would think so: BFD. But I came of age before the internet, before porn was in your pocket, before naked selfies and that charming courting gesture called *the dick pic*. To which I say: Thank you, sweet baby Jesus.

My children had a wonderful babysitter, now graduated and gone. Erica's nice college boyfriend once told my husband that guys in his fraternity had never seen a woman with pubic hair. That's how thoroughly the internet has molded young people's sexuality. In porn, apparently, the male ejaculation is more visually dramatic if the female is hairless. And because young men got used to seeing bald female genitalia, women began waxing in order to meet this standard, a standard begot by the porn industry for the money shot.

Sometimes, it's so lovely to be irrelevant.

Yes, I know about professional artist's models, muses like Jane Avril and Dora Maar. But neither Avril nor Maar lived in the Bible Belt. Around here, you can get reprimanded for cursing during pickleball.

Rob has offered me an artist's print of my portrait on some fancy deckle-edged paper, which is very kind—I hadn't known that would be part of the deal. I want it, this print. But I have no idea what I'll do with it. I certainly can't hang it. My sons would pack up their Legos and Nerf guns and run away.

On second thought, maybe I'll hang it.

As for the original being out in the world, I take comfort both from its size and its price, which ensure that it won't be centered over my ex-boyfriend's couch anytime soon (eat your heart out, Colin). Apparently, I can bear strangers in Berlin or Stockholm seeing the portrait in a museum and saying, "That's art." Can't bear some local nineteen-year-old seeing it in a coffee shop and saying, "Dude, that's my English professor."

The curse of being a professor is that if I do my job well, eventually I'm superfluous. Each May, my students flood out into the world and I stay put.

Sometimes a student comes along you can't let gallop off into the sunset. Such was the case with Molly McCully Brown. Molly was young when we first met, but wiser than any other twenty-year-old. Than any forty-year-old. Molly has cerebral palsy, which might have something to do with her old soul—she's spent a lot of time in pain. Anyway, we were ready for each other. We transitioned from mentor-student to friend-friend.

This summer, Molly visited for a few days, and one night after dinner we were talking on our porch. My laptop was within reach. I slowly dragged it close, making a decision: "I have something to show you."

I'd revealed the photo of my portrait to no one save my husband.

Why? I think I felt an urge to protect the purity of an experience that would evaporate when exposed to air. Rather like the time after I've written a poem and before I've sent it out for publication. A private time, free from adjudication. After the poem is published, it belongs to the reader to love or hate or misinterpret. It belongs to the reader, which is the dream of art. But before it belongs to the reader, it's mine in a way it will never be again.

As with the portrait: Rob will hang the seven-foot-tall me on a wall, and after he does, I'll belong to the viewer. But before then, I'm my secret to spill.

I spilled.

I pulled up the image and in silence we studied it, the cicadas seeming loud. Molly said something like "Wow." I lowered my pinched fingers to the touchpad—I couldn't help myself—American culture has schooled me well—and drew them out to enlarge my belly. Together we studied that stretched, poochy skin around my navel.

"Well," I sighed at last, "it's the stomach of a fifty-one-year-old woman who's had three kids."

"Yes. Yes, it is," said Molly, but with a tone quite unlike mine—not of resignation but of affirmation. "It's the stomach of a fifty-one-year-old woman who's had three kids."

And then we turned from the laptop toward each other and smiled.

See, I told you she was wise.

For why should I wish to appear otherwise? Nothing in my life has transformed me as much as becoming a mother. Why wouldn't I want my exterior to show signs of this interior transformation? Why would I think—why would I hope—I could erase the evidence?

Fun fact: The person most responsible for my stretched tummy is my middle child. He came out two weeks late and ten pounds fat, a monster who nearly killed me eighteen years ago in this very house where I'm writing these words, a home birth gone bad that landed me in the ER, unconscious and hemorrhaging. (In case you're wondering, I've forgiven him.) The wonderful woman who was my doula that long day's night would become, I'd later discover, another of the Oxford 12.

Rob hasn't exhibited the entire Oxford 12 together yet—to do so will be a massive undertaking. One idea he's had for the exhibition is that attendees must also be naked, which would strip the power differential between viewer and viewed. Perhaps when vulnerability is a burden shared by all, it ceases to be a burden. Perhaps it becomes a gift.

Remember Rob's question: What makes us human?

Maybe perceiving each other's humanity makes us human. Recognizing ourselves in each other. Acknowledging our collaboration in the great human experiment.

When confronting my own portrait, I become more human to myself. I am so clearly visible. What would be the point, now, in masquerading as another, or as a perfected version of myself? Isn't that the lesson of Helen's radical self-acceptance? It's too late for me to seek shelter through filters and Photoshop, too late for avoidant poses and diffused light to distract, correct, or erase. I'm reminded that at all times—not just while confronting my portrait—I am nakedly human, flawed and alive.

To prove it, I went on the record. For this one bright brief moment on planet Earth, framed in fluorescent pink, I was alive.

Dear viewer of my naked body,

Enjoy the bunions.

Acknowledgments

Thank you to the magazines in which these pieces first appeared, sometimes in alternate versions and with different titles.

Action, Spectacle: "Birthday," "Fennessy," "The Hug," "Prepping to Teach O'Connor While Visiting My Mother-in-Law," and "Two Sisters, One Slicing the Cake, One Choosing First"

Arkansas International: "Flughafen Tempelhof"

Brevity: "Me vs. Slugs: Pandemic Edition"

Brink: "This Little Trick I Play on Myself" and "Strangers with Good Taste, That Is"

Cincinnati Review: "Lori Cornelius" and "The Trespass"

Kenyon Review: "It Is Hard When Your Job Is Hard but Doesn't Appear to Be So," "My Sister Used to Give Me Blank Journals for My Birthday," "Only the Basement," "Two Sisters, One Fast, One Slow," "The Irish Goodbye," and "Related Searches"

Missouri Review: "Making Plans with Friends" and "Married Love: Addendum to 'Making Plans with Friends'"

Ninth Letter: "Lullaby"

Notre Dame Magazine: "The Roomies" and "My Mother-in-Law in the Mirror"

Notre Dame Review: "A Woman's Head Is Not the Safest Place to Be," "Dad Gave Us Twenty Dollars, Which Was a Lot in 1979," "While You Were Out," and "What I Think About When Someone Says They're Estranged from Their Sibling"

Oxford American: "Being Sensitive About Being Sensitive," "Married Love: Because I've Been French Kissing Him for Twenty-Nine Years," "Married Love: Missing Him," "Married Love: Playing the Long Game," and "Married Love: Twenty-Fifth Anniversary"

Ploughshares: "The Stories We Tell About the Stories We Tell"

Poetry: "Two Sisters, One Thinner, One Better Dressed"

Post Road: "Elegy," "Character Witness," and "Inheritance"

River Teeth: "Because My Editor Suggests I Reveal How My Sister Died"

Southern Indiana Review: "Married Love: Double Dating," "Married Love: Rolf und Helga," "Tree Pose," "Number One Sign You Shouldn't Send That Letter," and "Most Days Are Days like This"

Washington Post: "A Scrap of Paper That Says *Remember*"

"My Sister Used to Give Me Blank Journals for My Birthday" was reprinted in *Short Reads*.

"A Scrap of Paper That Says *Remember*" was reprinted in *Root Cause: Stories of Health, Harm, and Reclaiming Our Humanity in an Epidemic of Loneliness*.

"This Little Trick I Play on Myself" and "Strangers with Good Taste, That Is" were reprinted in *Malleable and True: A Hybrid Craft Anthology*, Brink Books.

"Flughafen Tempelhof" was reprinted in the American Academy in Berlin newsletter.

"Related Searches" and "Me vs. Slugs" were reprinted in *The Best of the Shortest: A Southern Writers Reading Reunion*, Livingston Press.

"Two Sisters, One Thinner, One Better Dressed" was reprinted as a broadside for the Public Poetry Initiative's *The Elegy Project*, and included in *Poetry Studio: Prompts for Poets*, University of Akron Press, and *The Columbia Granger's World of Poetry*.

"The Stories We Tell About the Stories We Tell" was reprinted in *A Second Blooming: Becoming the Women We Are Meant to Be*, Mercer University Press.
"Dear Viewer of My Naked Body" won The Shelby Foote Essay Prize, awarded by The Pirate's Alley Faulkner Society.

Ardent thanks to the following writing residencies: AIR Serenbe, Georgia, for the Focus Fellowship; the Betsy–South Beach for the SWIMM Residency; Château de Lavigny, Switzerland, for the Ledig-Rowohlt Fellowship; and the Loghaven Foundation, Tennessee, for a Loghaven Fellowship. This book benefited hugely from the uninterrupted time to write and reflect that these sanctuaries offered. And I wouldn't have been able to take advantage of them without my husband, Tom Franklin, who made it possible because he not only cheerfully took on solo parenting but also cared for my mother in my absence.

Thanks to the College of Liberal Arts at the University of Mississippi for a sabbatical, and to the following grant organizations: South Arts, for an Individual Artist Career Opportunity Grant; the Mississippi Arts Commission, for Individual Artist Grants in Nonfiction and Poetry; and the Academy of American Poets, for a Laureate Fellowship. Both the financial support and the encouragement boosted me tremendously.

Every writer should be so lucky as to have four warrior-poets in her corner. Thank you, Molly McCully Brown, Ann Fisher-Wirth, Melissa Ginsburg, and Aimee Nezhukumatathil, for reading this manuscript. When I wrote in "The Roomies" that "my colleagues are great," I meant y'all, and the MFA program, and the English Department at the University of Mississippi, where I've been fortunate to teach talented students since 2002. Late in the writing of this book, my mom fell and broke her hip. The chair of my department, Caroline Wigginton, made it possible for me to take personal leave to be by my mom's side. Thank you, Caroline. I'll never not be grateful that I was able to be with my mom when she needed me.

Thank you, forever roomies: Laura Hajdukiewicz, Denise Chabot Karkos, Beth Louder, Carmen Lund Nanni. Thanks, honorary roomie, Lloyd Adams. Thanks, *kamarádka* Kathleen Ziegler, for adventures and nougat. Thanks, Rob Townsend, for bringing your revelatory talent to our town. Thanks, Pat Lippens—I'm so glad that, thirty-six years ago, that foreign exchange program placed you in my house (and in my heart). For conversations about the writing life, thanks, David Wright Faladé, Michael Downs, Laura Lippman, Erika Randall, Erika Meitner, John T. Edge, and Jack Sonni, whom I dearly miss. Blair Hobbs and Rosie McDavid, your friendship enriches my life daily in ways too numerous to count. To Oxford: Stay square. To Square Books: Thanks for being the best corner in the universe.

Huge thanks to my fabulous agent, Judith Weber, and her husband, Nat Sobel—you two are like family to Tommy and me. Everyone at Sobel Weber Associates deserves a lifetime supply of sequins and salted caramels. Thanks to Anya Backlund of my speaking agency, Blue Flower Arts, for her nimble assistance. Thank you to Jill Bialosky, my editor, who did indeed prod me to write a piece that this book needed and which I was reluctant to write, and whose sage counsel in all matters literary has been an undeniable blessing. It's been a dream to be on Team Norton for six books, and I thank MVP Laura Mucha (Mucha appreciated!) as well as Amy Robbins, Ramona Wilkes, Don Rifkin, Meredith McGinnis, Sarahmay Wilkinson, and the always-awesome Erin Sinesky Lovett.

Thanks to my kids, Anna Claire, Thomas, and Nolan. Being y'all's mom is the great gift of my life. Also: Sorry about the portrait.

One more time, because you're first and last, Tommy, best friend, best reader, best luck I ever had. Without you, nothing gold. Keep folding the oven mitts.